GREEK WORD STUDIES FOR EVERYONE

GREEK WORD STUDIES FOR EVERYONE

An **Easy** Guide to **Serious** Study of the Bible

Benjamin L. **Merkle** and Robert L. **Plummer**

ACADEMIC®
BRENTWOOD, TENNESSEE

Published by B&H Academic®
Brentwood, Tennessee

ISBN: 978-1-0877-7888-4

Dewey Decimal Classification: 220.48
Subject Heading: GREEK LANGUAGE, BIBLICAL \ GREEK LANGUAGE, BIBLICAL--READERS \ GREEK LANGUAGE, BIBLICAL--GRAMMAR

Cover design by Kristen Ingebretson. Cover illustrations by Shutterstock, Hand-drawn Greek alphabet and ancient broken statues.

Printed in the United States of America

2 3 4 5 6 7 8 9 10 VP 30 29 28 27 26 25

CONTENTS

//////////////////

ABBREVIATIONS

//////////////////

BDAG	*A Greek-English Lexicon of the New Testament and Other Early Christian Literature*, 3rd ed., University of Chicago Press, 2000.
EGGNT	Exegetical Guide to the Greek New Testament
GNT	Greek New Testament
Louw & Nida	Louw, Johannes P., and Eugene A. Nida. *Greek-English Lexicon of the New Testament Based on Semantic Domains*, 2 vols. New York: United Bible Societies, 1988.
LXX	Septuagint (the Greek translation of the Old Testament)
NIDNTTE	*New International Dictionary of New Testament Theology and Exegesis*. 5 vols. Grand Rapids: Zondervan, 2014.
NT	New Testament
OT	Old Testament

HOW TO USE THIS BOOK

//////////////////

This book is designed to be used with the free video resources keyed to the book at https://www.wordstudiesforeveryone.com. Before reading each chapter, you should watch the overview video on the website. Then, after reading and studying the chapter, attempt the practice exercises on your own. Finally, check your answers by viewing the practice exercise videos at https://www.wordstudiesforeveryone.com. Also, at this website you will find a link to free digital flashcards to help you memorize the lists of Greek vocabulary words in each chapter.

This book is ideal for use in a small group setting of a local church. The facilitator need not have prior knowledge of Greek, but a pastor or church staff member who has studied Greek at a college or seminary may be the most natural leader. Pastor, leading others in a study of Greek is a great way to revive your own skills!

We want to thank the volunteers who read drafts of this manuscript and offered feedback, including Lauren Lockhart and Faith Steele. Special thanks to Mark Schisler for some of the images used in the video resources. Thank you to the excellent volunteer proofreaders Trevor Barylske, Daniel Kunkel, Christian Hedland, and Tyler Ziemer. Christian Hedland also gathered eleven pages of word study fallacies in preparation for this volume. We envisioned having repeated shaded sections interspersed throughout the volume, entitled "Don't Do This." We decided, however, not to include such sidebars, and we have attempted not to malign any pastors or other Christians in discussing word study fallacies.

We frequently run into laypeople who are excited about doing Greek word studies yet unaware of the difficulty of such studies and unable to access the best resources. We hope this volume rectifies those deficiencies and that God's Word rings forth from his people ever more clearly and loudly because of the instruction in this textbook.

Benjamin L. Merkle
Robert L. Plummer

Use the following link and QR code to access the video resources:

wordstudiesforeveryone.com

CHAPTER 1

//////////////////

YOU CAN READ EVERY WORD IN THE GREEK NEW TESTAMENT TODAY!

We recommend watching the video lecture before reading the chapter. The QR code and link to the video can be found on page x.

1.1 OVERVIEW

It is tempting to dive right into Greek word study tools; but you need to be able to read Greek words before we talk about what those words mean. For many of you, this is the place where you go from the JV to the Varsity team. It's time to stop pretending you were reading Greek and really learn to do so.

In this opening chapter, we will introduce you to the Greek alphabet as well as how to pronounce the various letters and letter combinations. We will also explain breathing marks, accent marks, and punctuation marks. Are such terms completely new to you? Don't worry. We are here to guide you. Your joyful journey of doing informed word studies on the Greek New Testament (GNT) is about to begin! At the end of this chapter, you will be able to read every word in the GNT! Now, let's be honest; you won't know the meaning of those words, but being able to pronounce and write them is a huge step that will open up the best Greek word study resources to you. If you are content to continue reading Greek only in *transliteration* (Greek words written with the Latin/English alphabet) and are satisfied with less than the best resources, we want to challenge that complacency and call you to a deeper study of the Bible.

1.2 SIGNIFICANCE

In this chapter, you will learn the letters of the Greek alphabet. Did you know that a single Greek letter can make a difference in interpretation? The Greek text of James 2:14 looks like this:

> Τί τὸ ὄφελος, ἀδελφοί μου, ἐὰν <u>πίστιν</u> λέγῃ τις ἔχειν, ἔργα δὲ μὴ ἔχῃ; μὴ δύναται **ἡ** <u>πίστις</u> σῶσαι αὐτόν;

An English translation (ESV) reads this way:

> What good is it, my brothers, if someone says he has <u>faith</u> but does not have works? Can **that** <u>faith</u> save him?

The bold Greek letter toward the end of the verse is an eta (**ἡ**). It looks much like the English letter "n." This one-letter word is the Greek *article* (i.e., similar to "the" in English), but it also has other functions. One function is called "the article of previous reference." That is, in some contexts, it can serve to mark a previous reference to the same noun (which usually appears the first time without an article). Note above how the first (underlined) instance of faith (πίστιν, *pistin*) does not have an eta in front of it, but the second (also underlined) appearance of the word (πίστις, *pistis*) does. This use of eta allows the writer to say, in effect, "the kind of faith I just mentioned above." Observe the apt translation of the ESV above ("that faith"). Of course, interpretations based on Greek grammatical observations should always be further supported by the surrounding context, as this interpretation is. Not translating the noun "faith" with an explicit marker for previous reference in English (e.g., "such" or "that") introduces the possibility of significant theological misunderstanding. Note the wording of the King James Version (KJV):

> What doth it profit, my brethren, though a man say he hath faith, and have not works? can faith save him?

In reading this translation, one could wrongly conclude that faith cannot save. James actually says that a *false* faith characterized by an empty verbal profession ("that faith") is unable to save. One Greek letter can make a significant difference in interpretation.

1.3 ALPHABET

LOWER CASE	UPPER CASE	LETTER NAME	ERASMIAN PRONUNCIATION	RECONSTRUCTED KOINE GREEK[1] PRONUNCIATION	MODERN PRONUNCIATION
α	Α	Alpha	f**a**ther		
β	Β	Beta	**b**all	Ha**b**ana **v**ault	**v**ault
γ	Γ	Gamma	**g**ift	**gh**oul **y**es	**gh**oul **y**es
δ	Δ	Delta	**d**og	**dh**	**dh**, **th**at
ε	Ε	Epsilon	**e**cho		
ζ	Ζ	Zeta	ku**dz**u	**z**oo	**z**oo
η	Η	Eta	**a**te	P**e**dro	**e**at
θ	Θ	Theta	**th**in		
ι	Ι	Iota	s**i**t (short) sk**i** (long)	sk**i**	sk**i**
κ	Κ	Kappa	**k**ey		
λ	Λ	Lambda	**l**ock		
μ	Μ	Mu	**m**om		
ν	Ν	Nu	**n**ail		
ξ	Ξ	Xi	fo**x**		
ο	Ο	Omicron	**o**ften	**o**bey	**o**bey
π	Π	Pi	**p**ond	s**p**ill	**p**ond **b**ond
ρ	Ρ	Rho	**rh**yme		
σ / ς	Σ	Sigma	**s**and		
τ	Τ	Tau	**t**ap	s**t**ill	**t**oe **d**oe
υ	Υ	Upsilon	b**oo**t	German "**ü**"	b**ea**t
φ	Φ	Phi	**ph**one		
χ	Χ	Chi	a**ch**e	German "**ch**"	a**ch**e **h**ue
ψ	Ψ	Psi	oo**ps**		
ω	Ω	Omega	**o**bey		

[1] This is adapted from Randall Buth, "Notes on the Pronunciation System of Koine Greek," https://www.biblicallanguagecenter.com/wp-content/uploads/2012/08/Koine-Pronunciation-2012.pdf.

1.4 PRONUNCIATION

Since you are reading a textbook written in English, it's likely you have never thought deeply about ideographic languages, such as Chinese, which use tiny pictures (or *ideographs*) to convey meaning. To be competent in reading such a language, one must learn thousands of characters. English and Greek, on the other hand, employ a limited number of symbols (twenty-six and twenty-four, respectively) to create a phonetic approximation of spoken speech. The famous biblical archaeologist W. F. Albright (1891–1971) once quipped about the Hebrew alphabet, "Since the forms of the letters are very simple, the 22-letter alphabet could be learned in a day or two by a bright student and in a week or two by the dullest."[2] We take alphabets for granted, but their introduction was revolutionary—akin to the introduction of the smartphone in more recent history. Even if you feel that you are a dull language student (we all feel that way sometimes), you can definitely learn the Greek alphabet in one or two weeks, at most. Many of you will learn the Greek alphabet in a couple of hours.

Scholars debate the best way to pronounce Koine Greek, which is Greek used from roughly 300 BC to AD 330 and the language in which the New Testament was penned. We follow a pronunciation system ultimately derived from Desiderius Erasmus (1466–1536). This system is used by most Greek professors and has the benefit of clearly differentiating the various vowel sounds. In

> *DESIDERIUS ERASMUS* (1466–1536) published the first printed Greek New Testament in 1516. He wrote, "It was not for empty fame or childish pleasure that in my youth I grasped at the polite literature of the ancients, and by late hours gained some slight mastery of Greek and Latin. It has been my cherished wish to cleanse the Lord's temple of barbarous ignorance, and to adorn it with treasures brought from afar, such as may kindle in hearts a warm love for the Scriptures." —Erasmus, *Enchiridion Militis Christiani* (1501)

[2] Carl H. Kraeling and R. M. Adams, eds., *City Invincible: A Symposium on Urbanization and Cultural Development in the Ancient Near East* (Chicago: University of Chicago Press, 1960), 123.

contrast, modern Greek is pronounced such that eta (η), iota (ι), and upsilon (υ) all have the same sound.

Some scholars advocate pronouncing Koine Greek the same way as modern Greek because we do not know precisely how Koine Greek was pronounced. Others argue for a "reconstructed Koine" pronunciation based on a study of spelling mistakes made by ancient scribes. There are benefits and limitations to any pronunciation scheme. The videos keyed to this book use Erasmian pronunciation, but if you are in a small group study led by an instructor who uses a different pronunciation, we recommend you use his or her pronunciation system.

Note that sigma has two forms. The first form (σ) is used at the beginning (<u>σ</u>ύν) and middle (πί<u>σ</u>τιν) of a word. The final sigma (ς) is used if it is the last letter of a word (λόγο<u>ς</u>).

The Greek alphabet has twenty-four letters. Perhaps you will find it easier to learn them in six groups of four:

α β γ δ	ν ξ ο π
ε ζ η θ	ρ σ/ς τ υ
ι κ λ μ	φ χ ψ ω[3]

One of the most effective ways to learn a new language's alphabet is with a song. Use the QR codes or web links in this book to access additional audio and video resources, including a version of the Greek alphabet song.

Five Greek letters are considered *double consonants* since they require the use of two letters when transliterated: θ (th), ξ (xs), φ (ph), χ (ch), and ψ (ps). Transliteration means writing one language phonetically (that is, writing out its sounds) with another language's letters or characters.

The letter gamma (γ), by itself, is always pronounced with a hard *g* (as in "goat" but never like "giraffe"). When placed before certain other consonants (γ, κ, ξ, χ), it is pronounced with an "n" sound. For example, ἄγγελος is pronounced án-ge-los (not ág-ge-los).

Pay attention, since some letters are easy to confuse with others:

γ → ν   ζ → ξ   θ → φ   κ → χ   ν → υ   ο → σ   π → τ   φ → ψ

---

[3] Hint: The letter's name includes the sound of the letter. For example, the letter beta makes the "b" sound found in the name of the letter (*<u>b</u>eta*).

Moreover, you will soon notice that Greek fonts differ slightly from each other. The difference seems huge to some beginning students, but in a short time, you will barely notice the slight variations—just as you likely don't consciously think about the differences between the Times New Roman and Courier fonts. Even if you are one of those aesthetically sensitive people who does notice the differences in English fonts, you are neither confused nor troubled by them. Handwritten Greek letters also look slightly different from their printed versions, just as handwritten Latin/English letters look different from the printed Times New Roman font. Don't let those differences bother you. Rely on the accompanying video lecture to teach you how to handwrite the Greek alphabet. You must learn to write it. You must practice writing Greek words. Now, when you doodle on your church bulletin, you should be writing Greek words.

Be careful because some Greek letters closely resemble letters in the English alphabet.

η (eta) → "n"	ρ (rho) → "p"	χ (chi) → "x"
ν (nu) → "v"	υ (upsilon) → "u"	ω (omega) → "w"

1.5 VOWELS

Linguists classify vowel sounds as "long" or "short" based on how long it originally took to pronounce them relative to other vowels in the same language. This time difference is not something you will be able to distinguish by listening to Greek and is somewhat hypothetical based on where and how the vowels are articulated in the mouth. These labels of "short" and "long," however, will become important later if you continue your study in Greek. For now, learn this: there are seven vowels in Greek: α, ε, η, ι, ο, υ, and ω. Some of these vowels are considered short (α, ε, ι, ο, υ) and others are considered long (α, η, ι, υ, ω). Note that the vowels α, ι, and υ can be either short or long. If you continue in your Greek study after this book, you will learn that vowels can sometimes lengthen (shift from short to long) when changes are made to a word.[4] Here is a chart demonstrating how short vowels lengthen:

---

[4] The technical term for vowels that change their length (short → long or long → short) is *ablaut*.

Short		**Long**		**Short/Long**
ε	→	η	←	α
ο	→	ω		ι
				υ

When the letter iota (ι) follows the long vowels α, η, and ω, it is frequently written underneath that vowel and is not pronounced. This is called an *iota subscript*: καρδίᾳ, ἀγάπῃ, λόγῳ. You will not have to decide whether to make the iota a subscript. It will just be part of the spelling of the word or form you are memorizing or reading.

1.6 DIPHTHONGS

A *diphthong* (from the Greek word διφθόγγος, meaning "having two sounds") is two vowels together that are pronounced as one sound.

LOWER CASE	PRONUNCIATION
αι	**ai**sle
αυ	kr**au**t
ει	fr**ei**ght
ευ	f**eu**d
οι	**oi**l
ου	s**ou**p
υι	s**ui**te

When two vowels are together yet not a diphthong, a *diaeresis mark* (i.e., two raised dots above the vowel: ϊ, ϋ) is frequently placed above the second vowel to signal that the two vowels are pronounced separately (cf. the English word *naïve*).[5] This mark is most commonly found on *proper nouns* (names and places—especially those imported from Hebrew or Aramaic) and usually occurs above an iota (e.g., Κάϊν = Kah-een, "Cain"; Μωϋσῆς = Mō-oo-seys, "Moses"; Ἑβραϊστί

[5] *Diaeresis* is pronounced die-AIR-eh-sis. In other languages, two dots above a vowel can have a different function, as the umlaut does in German. Although it is important for us to note them, diaeresis marks are uncommon.

= Heh-bra-ees-tee, "in Hebrew/Aramaic"). Other vowel combinations don't form diphthongs and are also pronounced separately (e.g., ηυ = ay-oo; ιε = ee-eh, and ιη = ee-ay). Because this last vowel combination (ιη) is used to mirror the Hebrew/ Aramaic *yod* sound, the vowels are typically pronounced together ("yea"). Thus, the name for "Jesus" is Ἰησοῦς and is pronounced "yea-soos."

1.7 BREATHING MARKS

Every Greek word that begins with a vowel (including a diphthong) is given a *breathing mark*. Writing a breathing mark is analogous to dotting the lowercase letter "i" in English. Most of the time, it does not affect pronunciation; the accepted conventions of writing the language just require it. There are two types of breathing marks: smooth and rough. With a smooth breathing mark (ʼ), the most common type, there is no change in pronunciation. With a rough breathing mark (ʽ), an "h" sound is added to the beginning of the word. If a word begins with a single uppercase (capital) vowel, the breathing mark is written to the left of that letter, at the top of the line (e.g., Ἀβαδδών, "Abaddon" or Ἡρῴδης, "Herod").[6] Also, if a word begins with a diphthong, the breathing mark appears over the second letter (αἷμα, "blood" or Αἴγυπτος, "Egypt"). An initial upsilon (υ) always has a rough breathing mark. The only consonant to receive a breathing mark is rho (ῥ), which also always includes a rough breathing mark. The "h" sound does not affect the pronunciation of rho but is evidenced in English words derived from Greek (e.g., rhetoric → ῥητορική).[7] In ancient Greek, the rough breathing mark over the rho was apparently a cue to the reader to trill the "r sound."

ἁμαρτία	→	hah-mar-teé-ah	"sin"
ἑπτά	→	hep-táh	"seven"
ἡμέρα	→	hey-mé-rah	"day"
ὁδός	→	haw-dáws	"way/road"

[6] Note that the initial capital Greek letter in the name Ἡρῴδης that looks like an English *H* is actually a capital eta—a vowel pronounced like the "ay" in the English word *may*. It is only the rough breathing mark that gives the Greek word Ἡρῴδης an initial "h" sound in pronunciation.

[7] If you have a Greek *lexicon* (dictionary), flip to the list of words that begin with rho (ρ) and note how few there are. Observe too how all the words that begin with rho have a rough breathing mark.

ὕδωρ	→	hoó-dōr	"water"
ὡσαννά	→	hō-san-náh	"hosanna"
ῥῆμα	→	ráy-mah	"word"

1.8 ACCENT MARKS

Most words in a modern GNT will have *accent marks*. According to tradition, it was the head of the library in Alexandria, Aristophanes of Byzantium (c. 257–180 BC), who first developed a system of accentuation to help non-native speakers pronounce Greek. In the second and third centuries BC, Greek was still a tonal language, with accents guiding speakers on rising and falling pitches. By the first century AD, when the NT was written, Greek likely had lost its tonality; thus, we should understand the accents as communicating stress or emphasis to the reader/speaker. That is, a reader should say the accented syllable a bit louder or longer, stressing or emphasizing it. For example, as we saw above, the word for "sin" is ἁμαρτία, pronounced "hah-mar-teé-ah." The accent mark signifies that the emphasis is given to the third syllable ("teé"). The presence and function of accents on words can also help readers know whether a vowel is long or short, which reveals the proper pronunciation. Accents are not found widely in Greek manuscripts until the fifth century AD and are lacking from the oldest manuscripts of the GNT.

We consistently stress certain syllables when we say English words, but we don't mark those syllables with accents. Can emphasizing a different syllable change meaning? You bet! Pronounce Indianapolis with the "an" stressed (IndiANapolis), and it sounds like you are saying "Indiana police," rather than the city, "IndiaNApolis."

Modern editions of the GNT have three different accent marks:

Acute	ά	→	ἀγάπη	ah-gá-pay
Grave[8]	ὰ	→	κεφαλὴ	keh-fa-láy
Circumflex	ᾶ	→	σοφῶν	saw-fóne

[8] Pronounced "grauve" like the color "mauve." If you view the grave accent as a small picture, it's like a slide going down into the grave (tomb). This will help you remember its pronunciation.

Accent marks can only be placed on a word's last three syllables. The names of these syllables are the (1) antepenult (before next-to-last syllable), (2) penult (next-to-last syllable), and (3) ultima (last syllable).

antepenult	penult	ultima
ἄν-	θρω-	πος

Your main focus on accents at this point should be to let them guide you in stressing the correct syllables when you read Greek aloud.[9]

1.9 PUNCTUATION MARKS

Punctuation marks are rarely found in Greek manuscripts written before the eighth century. In the earliest *extant* (that is, still existing) NT manuscripts, the script consists of all capital letters (*majuscule script*) that lacks spacing between words and has only rare, erratic punctuation. (Visit https://codexsinaiticus.org/en/ to view an important Christian codex [book version] of the Greek Bible from the early fourth century.) Over time, copies of the NT came to be written with lower case letters (*miniscule script*) and spacing between words. Eventually, other editorial elements were added which today include paragraphs, indentations, and breaks between clauses and sentences. Below is an example of John 1:1 in a format likely similar (though neater!) to how the apostle John originally penned it. This majuscule text is followed by the same words as they appear in most modern editions of the GNT:

ΕΝΑΡΧΗΗΝΟΛΟΓΟΣΚΑΙΟΛΟΓΟΣΗΝΠΡΟΣΤΟΝΘΕΟΝΚΑΙΘΕΟΣΗΝ ΟΛΟΓΟΣ

Ἐν ἀρχῇ ἦν ὁ λόγος, καὶ ὁ λόγος ἦν πρὸς τὸν θεόν, καὶ θεὸς ἦν ὁ λόγος.

"In the beginning was the Word, and the Word was with God, and the Word was God."

[9] For an accurate and accessible introduction to Greek accents, we recommend John A. K. Lee's *Basics of Greek Accents: Eight Lessons with Exercises* (Grand Rapids: Zondervan, 2018).

Modern Greek editions of the NT do not capitalize the first word of each sentence. Capitalization usually occurs (1) in the title of NT books (with every letter capitalized), and in the first letter of (2) *proper nouns*, (3) direct quotations, and (4) words that begin a new paragraph. Here are the punctuation marks commonly used in most modern editions of the GNT:

Period (.)	.	α.
Comma (,)	,	α,
Semicolon (;)	·	α·
Question Mark (?)	;	α;

1.10 VOCABULARY

In this textbook, we present seven new vocabulary words at the end of every chapter except chapter 7. By the end of this book, you will know forty-two Greek words!

The vocabulary words listed appear in their *lexical forms* (i.e., the dictionary forms). Another term for a dictionary is a lexicon. Below, each Greek term is given at least one English *gloss* (i.e., a brief English equivalent of the Greek term). Be mindful that an English definition given is merely one of many possible renderings. When we start using a lexicon later in this book, you will see how a good dictionary informs the user of the possible range of meaning of a particular word. Greek lexicons focused on the NT will often list particular instances in the NT, with the editors of the lexicons having made judgments on context-specific meanings.

One of the most helpful ways to learn new Greek vocabulary words is to note English *cognates,* that is, English words that can be traced to a Greek ancestral form. English cognates will be in parentheses alongside English definitions. If a Greek word does not list any English cognates, or the cognates are not familiar to you, you are advised to create your own memory device.

For example, the word ἁμαρτία (hah-mar-teé-ah) means "sin." Those who know the term *hamartiology* from broader theological reading should have no trouble remembering the meaning of ἁμαρτία. Most beginning Greek students, however, do not know such a rare, specialized word. So, you may need to make your own memory device based on associations and visual images related to the sound of the vocabulary word. When pronounced, the word ἁμαρτία sounds sort of like "hammer tea-a," so you can imagine sinning against your mother by smashing her favorite teacup with a hammer. In fact, the more memorable, shocking, and visual an association is, the better. So, involve all your senses. You can even act out walking to a table, closing your eyes, raising your arm, and seeing yourself smash the teacup with a hammer. As you do, say ἁμαρτία. Then imagine your poor mother looking at you in amazement, pointing her trembling, outstretched finger at you and yelling, "Sin!" After all, the most effective memory devices are the ones you create!

For further help in creative methods to learn Greek, we recommend another book we penned: *Greek for Life: Strategies for Learning, Retaining, and Reviving New Testament Greek* (Grand Rapids: Baker Academic, 2017). For a set of Greek vocabulary flashcards with a mnemonic device for each word, see *Beginning with New Testament Greek Vocabulary and Paradigm Cards* (Brentwood, TN: B&H Academic, 2024). We also suggest this helpful free website that includes a section on learning foreign language vocabulary: https://mullenmemory.com. Furthermore, we suggest you watch the video instruction keyed to this chapter and learn to handwrite Greek confidently. Perhaps create your own flashcards for the Greek words below and try to learn the meaning "both ways." So, for example, if I show you the Greek word ἀγάπη, you should be able to tell me it means "love." Likewise, if I ask you what the Greek word is for "love," you should be able to handwrite ἀγάπη. Always be sure to have a breathing mark on a word that begins with a vowel or diphthong, but don't worry about memorizing the placement of the accents.

ἀγάπη	love [noun]
ἀλήθεια	truth
ἁμαρτία	sin (hamartiology—the theological study of sin) [noun]
βασιλεία	kingdom, reign (basilica)
καρδία	heart (cardiologist)
δέ	and, but, now
καί	and, even, also

1.11 PRACTICE EXERCISES[10]

A. **Alphabet**: Memorize the Greek alphabet. The easiest way to do this is to learn to sing it (e.g., to the tune of "Twinkle, Twinkle, Little Star"). You'll know you have it when you can write out the lowercase script of the alphabet in the correct order and form ten times from memory.

α β γ δ – ε ζ η θ – ι κ λ μ – ν ξ ο π – ρ σ/ς τ υ – φ χ ψ ω

B. **Writing**: Handwrite the following Greek words. Practice writing them multiple times on a separate sheet of paper.

ἀγάπη ________________
ἀλήθεια ________________
ἁμαρτία ________________
βασιλεία ________________
καρδία ________________
δέ ________________
καί ________________

C. **Reading**: Read aloud John 3:14–21, paying close attention to accent and breathing marks. Although you will not yet understand what the words mean, learning to read Greek out loud is vital. It is very difficult to learn, understand, or translate words that you cannot pronounce. For thousands of free videos in which the professor (one of the authors of this textbook) reads a Greek verse aloud, go to https://dailydoseofgreek.com.

Καὶ καθὼς Μωϋσῆς ὕψωσεν τὸν ὄφιν ἐν τῇ ἐρήμῳ, οὕτως ὑψωθῆναι δεῖ τὸν υἱὸν τοῦ ἀνθρώπου, ἵνα πᾶς ὁ πιστεύων ἐν αὐτῷ ἔχῃ ζωὴν αἰώνιον. Οὕτως γὰρ ἠγάπησεν ὁ θεὸς τὸν κόσμον, ὥστε τὸν υἱὸν τὸν μονογενῆ

[10] Videos featuring a textbook author working through the practice exercises are found at https://www.wordstudiesforeveryone.com. Before accessing those videos, you should (1) study the material in this chapter and (2) attempt the activities without reference to the videos. We want to acknowledge with gratitude S. M. Baugh's influence on our organization of the "Practice" portion of the chapters into subsections that focus on specific skills.

ἔδωκεν, ἵνα πᾶς ὁ πιστεύων εἰς αὐτὸν μὴ ἀπόληται ἀλλ᾽ ἔχῃ ζωὴν αἰώνιον. οὐ γὰρ ἀπέστειλεν ὁ θεὸς τὸν υἱὸν εἰς τὸν κόσμον ἵνα κρίνῃ τὸν κόσμον, ἀλλ᾽ ἵνα σωθῇ ὁ κόσμος δι᾽ αὐτοῦ. ὁ πιστεύων εἰς αὐτὸν οὐ κρίνεται· ὁ δὲ μὴ πιστεύων ἤδη κέκριται, ὅτι μὴ πεπίστευκεν εἰς τὸ ὄνομα τοῦ μονογενοῦς υἱοῦ τοῦ θεοῦ. αὕτη δέ ἐστιν ἡ κρίσις ὅτι τὸ φῶς ἐλήλυθεν εἰς τὸν κόσμον καὶ ἠγάπησαν οἱ ἄνθρωποι μᾶλλον τὸ σκότος ἢ τὸ φῶς· ἦν γὰρ αὐτῶν πονηρὰ τὰ ἔργα. πᾶς γὰρ ὁ φαῦλα πράσσων μισεῖ τὸ φῶς καὶ οὐκ ἔρχεται πρὸς τὸ φῶς, ἵνα μὴ ἐλεγχθῇ τὰ ἔργα αὐτοῦ· ὁ δὲ ποιῶν τὴν ἀλήθειαν ἔρχεται πρὸς τὸ φῶς, ἵνα φανερωθῇ αὐτοῦ τὰ ἔργα ὅτι ἐν θεῷ ἐστιν εἰργασμένα.

CHAPTER 2

//////////////////

WORD STUDIES CAN BE DANGEROUS

We recommend watching the video lecture before reading the chapter. The QR code and link to the video can be found on page x.

2.1 OVERVIEW

Many well-meaning pastors and Christian authors have perpetuated flawed approaches to Greek word studies. Greek word studies can be interesting and helpful, but they can also be dangerous. Similar to the way a good driver's training course will inform you of the dangers of hurtling down the interstate in a two-ton piece of metal, this chapter will warn you of the dangers of doing Greek word studies poorly. (Having said that, we always want to start each chapter with a responsible approach to Greek word studies or Greek grammar, which you will find below in the significance section.)

2.2 SIGNIFICANCE

In Paul's letter to the Philippians, he employs two related words that convey the idea of "citizenship." In Philippians 1:27, the apostle wrote, "Whatever happens, conduct yourselves (πολιτεύεσθε, *politeuesthe*) in a manner worthy of the gospel of Christ" (NIV). With this translation, the New International Version obscures Paul's reference to citizenship. The Christian Standard Bible (CSB), on the other hand, makes the citizenship allusion explicit: "Just one thing: As citizens of heaven, live your life worthy of the gospel of Christ." Later, in Philippians 3:20, the apostle uses another "citizenship" word, with virtually all modern English Bible translations translating it so as to show the explicit allusion to citizenship. The CSB is typical: "Our citizenship (πολίτευμα, *politeuma*) is in heaven, and we eagerly wait for a Savior from there, the Lord Jesus Christ" (Phil 3:20). Joseph Hellerman insightfully notes that this concentration of citizenship terms in Paul's letter to the Philippians is not an accident. Indeed, in the narrative of Acts, only in Philippi does the issue of Paul's citizenship arise (Acts 16:37–39).[1] Moreover, as an official Roman colony, Philippi had certain privileges and rights that resulted in a higher percentage of the population being Roman citizens. According to Hellerman, an estimated 40 percent of the population at Philippi would have been citizens as compared to an estimated 14 percent of citizens in a city that was not a Roman colony.[2] Hellerman summarizes:

> We conclude that Paul intentionally employs this politically charged term (subversively, in view of the pride of honors associated with Roman citizenship in the colony) in reference to another citizen body, namely the Christian community in Philippi. . . . Paul intentionally marks out the church in the colony as an alternative society vis-à-vis the Roman imperial order. Readers are thereby prepared for the politically provocative acclamation of Jesus—not Caesar—as κύριος [*kurios*, Lord] in [Phil] 2:11.[3]

So, Christian, citizen of heaven, where does your ultimate loyalty lie? In the governments and leaders of this world, or in your Lord and his kingdom?

2.3 POTENTIAL PERILS IN DOING GREEK WORK STUDIES

Below are some warnings you should keep in mind as you engage in Greek word studies.[4]

---

[1] Joseph H. Hellerman, *Philippians*, ed. Andreas J. Köstenberger and Robert W. Yarbrough, Exegetical Guide to the Greek New Testament (Nashville: B&H Academic, 2015), 78.

[2] Hellerman, 78.

[3] Hellerman, 78.

[4] Several of the paragraphs below are adapted from Andreas J. Köstenberger, Benjamin L. Merkle, and Robert L. Plummer, *Going Deeper with New Testament Greek: An Intermediate Study of the Grammar and Syntax of the New Testament*, rev. ed. (Nashville: B&H Academic, 2020), 483–99.

2.3.1 Do Not Confuse a Word's Range of Meaning with Its Specific, Contextually Determined Meaning.

All words have a range of meaning (*semantic range*). Let's first consider this reality in English. When I look up the word "sick" in the online Merriam-Webster Dictionary, it gives me these possible meanings:[5]

- affected with disease or ill health
- spiritually or morally unsound or corrupt
- sickened by strong emotion
- having a strong distaste from surfeit
- filled with disgust
- depressed and longing for something
- mentally or emotionally unsound or disordered
- highly distasteful
- lacking vigor
- badly outclassed
- incapable of producing profitable yields of a crop
- outstandingly or amazingly good or impressive (slang)

A list of definitions in the dictionary (if accurate and reflective of speakers' actual usage) gives us a word's semantic range, or range of meaning. How do we know, though, which of these meanings an author or speaker intends? We must consider the specific context in which a word was used. When a student tells me, "I can't come to class today because I am sick," even that short statement gives me sufficient context to determine that the student is using the word "sick" to mean "affected with disease or ill health" (bullet point one above).

Various errors can be made if a student fails to distinguish a word's range of meaning from its specific, contextually determined meaning. For example, the student can equate two different contexts and so wrongly transfer a word's correct contextually determined meaning from one setting to another. Again, it works best to illustrate these basic linguistic principles first in English. For example, imagine someone saying, "I put my faith in Jesus, and now I am saved!" Here, to be "saved" means to be rescued from eternal damnation. The same speaker (even

[5] https://www.merriam-webster.com/dictionary/sick, accessed October 25, 2023 (definitions slightly edited and condensed for presentation).

one moment later!) could say, "I was drowning in the pool, but the lifeguard saved me." No one listening to him would be confused and think that he also believes the lifeguard rescued him from eternal damnation.

This is an important point. It is wrong to assume an author/speaker means the same thing when using the same word, even when used in very close proximity. In saying the lifeguard "saved" him, the speaker does not mean the lifeguard rescued him from eternal damnation. He means the lifeguard rescued him from peril and kept him from drowning. We all intuitively understand that language works this way. If we import a word's context-specific meaning to a different setting without first making sure the literary contexts are similar, we can seriously distort the author's meaning. Linguist Martin Joos has summarized this linguistic principle with the influential phrase: "The least meaning is the best meaning."[6] This principle sounds odd at first, but after further thought, it makes sense.[7] Words all carry a variety of potential meanings, but the best understanding of any word's meaning is the one that least disturbs the broader literary context. The surrounding words and phrases prepare the reader to understand rightly any particular word. You cannot define a word in isolation. You cannot just extract the word "saved" from an English sentence and do a word study or define it. You must know the broader context in which the word appears. Consider the variety of meanings of "saved" in these short sentences:

- I **saved** three dollars by using this coupon.
- He **saved** me a seat at the movie theater.
- Jesus **saved** my soul from hell.
- The boy **saved** the little bird from the neighborhood cat.

Now, let's consider an example from the GNT. Have you ever heard someone declare that a faithful Bible translation consistently renders a Greek or Hebrew word with the same English word? Is that true? Consider applying that principle to the verses below. Each underlined word in English is a rendering of the same underlying Greek word, ἀφίημι (*aphiēmi*):

---

[6] This linguistic principle is also called "the rule of maximal redundancy." Cited in Moisés Silva, *Biblical Words and Their Meaning: An Introduction to Lexical Semantics*, rev. ed. (Grand Rapids: Zondervan, 1994), 153–54.

[7] Though I (Rob) did not consciously recall Silva's words when writing this paragraph, he makes nearly the same point (see Silva, *Biblical Words and Their Meaning*, 154).

- Jesus answered him, "Allow it for now, because this is the way for us to fulfill all righteousness." Then John allowed him to be baptized (Matt 3:15).
- Then the devil left him, and angels came and began to serve him (Matt 4:11).
- And forgive us our debts, as we also have forgiven our debtors (Matt 6:12).
- To the rest I say (I, not the Lord) that if any brother has a wife who is an unbeliever, and she consents to live with him, he should not divorce her (1 Cor 7:12 ESV).

The truth is that all words have a range of meaning, and it is essential to consider the surrounding context carefully to discern accurately the specific meaning. Always rendering a Greek word with the same English word would produce a strange translation and distort the inspired biblical author's meaning.

The linguistic fallacy of *illegitimate totality transfer* is another example of confusing a word's range of meaning with its specific, contextually determined meaning.[8] When a reader commits this fallacy, he illegitimately ascribes to a word the totality of what the word could mean in each individual instance of its usage. Many of us have heard preachers engage in this fallacy. For example, a pastor may say, "The Greek word in our text is κόσμος. I'm reading from a Greek dictionary now. It says κόσμος means 'adornment,' 'order,' 'the world,' 'the universe,' 'the sum total of all beings above the level of animals,' 'planet earth,' 'humanity,' 'the system of human existence in its many aspects,' and 'totality.'"[9] Of course, words do not mean the totality of what they could mean in any context; each word only means what the author cues the readers to understand in that particular literary setting. We see the foolishness of illegitimate totality transfer when we apply it to English. Imagine a preacher saying, "The man answered his cell phone. What does 'cell' mean? It means (a) a small chamber of incarceration, (b) a blob of protoplasm, (c) a mobile communications network, and (d) a square in a spreadsheet. How rich in meaning was this man's phone!"

---

[8] See D. A. Carson, *Exegetical Fallacies*, 2nd ed. (Grand Rapids: Baker, 1996), 53; Grant R. Osborne, *The Hermeneutical Spiral: A Comprehensive Introduction to Biblical Interpretation*, rev. and exp. (Downers Grove: InterVarsity, 2006), 84, 105; Andreas J. Köstenberger and Richard D. Patterson, *Invitation to Biblical Interpretation: Exploring the Hermeneutical Triad of History, Literature, and Theology*, Invitation to Theological Studies Series (Grand Rapids: Kregel Academic, 2011), 645–47.

[9] Various definitions taken from BDAG, 561–63.

2.3.2 When Seeking to Understand a Word's Range of Meaning, Do Not Look at Instances of the Word from Vastly Different Time Periods.[10]

All languages are in the process of changing. Language is like a rolling river that never stops, constantly picking up new influences and nuances. When you want to determine the possibilities of what a word could mean (its range of meaning), you need to look at the word being used in roughly the same time period. We have a much greater chance of rightly understanding a word's meaning if we rely on parallel uses from the same time period (i.e., synchronous uses).

Even in modern English, we can see how words have changed meaning over time. When I (Rob) looked up the word "sick" in the Merriam-Webster online dictionary for the writing of this chapter, the dictionary had a new entry that was not there ten years ago. "Sick" can now mean "outstandingly or amazingly good or impressive." If you are young or if you have teen children or grandchildren, you've likely heard this newer usage.

If you ever read an older English translation of the Bible, you are sure to encounter words that have changed meaning since the Bible's publication. The translators of the King James Version (published in 1611) rendered James 2:3 as: "Ye have respect to him that weareth the gay clothing, and say unto him, Sit thou here in a good place; and say to the poor, Stand thou there, or sit here under my footstool." In the early seventeenth century, the word "gay" meant "fine" or "luxurious." The word "gay" has experienced a dramatic semantic shift (change in meaning) over the last 400 years; its primary meaning now is "homosexual." In the same way, one must always remember that the words in the NT are a photograph of a moving target, that is, a snapshot of language in the process of change. For this reason, we should not cite Homer (c. eighth century BC) as the most authoritative source for the meaning of a NT Greek word, but we should rather seek sources contemporaneous with the writing of the NT to inform us. The best Greek lexicographers (scholars who compile dictionaries) understand this principle, and it informs their work.

A specific linguistic fallacy that fails to prioritize the same time period that the author/work under consideration is the *etymological fallacy*.[11] The etymologi-

---

[10] See Silva's helpful discussion in *Biblical Words and Their Meaning*, 35–38.

[11] For a discussion of the etymological fallacy, see Carson, *Exegetical Fallacies*, 28–33; Osborne, *Hermeneutical Spiral*, 84–89; Köstenberger and Patterson, *Invitation to Biblical Interpretation*, 631–35.

cal fallacy is the false claim that knowing the *etymology* (historical origins) of a word gives us deeper insights into its meaning. Many congregations are accustomed to being fed the etymological fallacy as part of their regular homiletical diet. Such supposed insights are introduced with phrases such as, "The Greek word here *really* means . . ." Congregations tolerate absurdities that would be laughable in their own language. For example, the English word "lasagna" comes from a Greek word *lasonon*, a small pot used as a portable bedroom toilet. How many of us have considered this etymology while enjoying a dish of baked pasta? The word "dandelion" comes from the French "*dent de lion*" (tooth of a lion). When you spray weed killer on the dandelions in your yard, do you imagine yourself as a lion tamer? Similarly, when the apostle Paul wrote a word, he was almost certainly not thinking about the origin of that word. He was unconsciously assuming the contemporary semantic range (range of meaning) and then narrowing that range further through cues in the surrounding literary context. This is an intuitive and unconscious process for native speakers of languages. Even as I (Rob) am typing this sentence, I am not listing off in my mind the possible meanings of my words and then consciously crafting the sentence to narrow the reader's perception to the proper understanding. Language does not work that way! When I read back through this paragraph, however, I will probably note a few places where my phrasing could be improved to guide the reader more directly to the point I am trying to make.

You may wonder how you will know whether the other Greek word usages you are looking at are from roughly the same time period as the NT. That's easy! We will only be using lexicons and resources that are focused broadly on the time of the NT. There are plenty of other Greek lexicons that focus on Greek from other time periods, and though some Greek words remain relatively constant in meaning over time, it would be wrong to assume a lexicon that focuses on Greek in the fifth century BC or fifth century AD would be reliable for the meaning of words at the time of the NT. Would you rely on an English dictionary from the 1600s to help you understand the meaning of English words today?

One of the most egregious examples of the etymological fallacy that I've ever heard didn't even employ proper etymology. A student brought me an article summarizing a session from a worship conference. The speaker at the conference noted that the Greek word for worship (προσκυνέω) was made up of a *prepositional prefix* (πρός) and a main part of the word (κυνέω). So far, he was right! He then asserted that the prefix πρός means "to/toward" (Again, correct.) and that the word κυνέω is the Greek verb for "dog." (Totally wrong. The Greek word for dog is κύων.) He proceeded to claim that this etymological analysis led him to conclude that we should approach God in the same way that a loyal canine bounds toward his master. Actually, the Greek word κυνέω means to kiss, so the word προσκυνέω probably originally had the connotation of bowing to kiss the ground, but by the time of the NT, the word meant simply to bow down or to worship.

In recent years, some biblical scholars have argued that the emphasis on considering the synchronous (same-time-period) uses of a biblical word have failed to account for biblical authors' reflections on the etymology of some words. This criticism is valid insofar as it points us to an ancient author's *consciously intended* allusion to a word's prior history. One must always ask: How has the biblical author led the reader to consider the origins or historical echoes in this word? For example, in Matthew 1:21, the Gospel author reports that an angel tells Joseph, "[Mary] will give birth to a son, and you are to name him Jesus, because he will save his people from their sins." Matthew clearly intends his audience to understand the etymological origin of Jesus's Hebrew name ("YHWH saves") as significant. In the Scriptures, biblical authors often viewed the etymological meaning of proper names as important. We know that fact because of the inspired authors' *explicit indications* in the text (e.g., Gen 25:26; 27:36; John 9:7–11).[12]

Another linguistic fallacy that looks to the wrong time period to understand Greek words is the *reverse etymological fallacy*. In the reverse etymological fallacy, the preacher or student allows modern words related to or derived from the Greek word to wrongly shape his or her understanding of the word. For example, a preacher may say, "Here in Romans 1:16, Paul uses the word δύναμις to describe the Gospel. Δύναμις is a word from which we derive the word 'dynamite.' The gospel is an explosive power just waiting to be revealed through your life!"

The English language is an Indo-European language related to Greek, so we can trace the etymology of many English words back to Greek. If you are trying to quickly learn Greek vocabulary, finding an English cognate will speed you along.

---

[12] Etymological studies are usually a last resort, often most helpful with rare words and proper names.

(For example, the Greek word for "heart" is καρδία, and we have many cognates of καρδία in English—cardiologist, cardiac, etc.) It would be a mistake, however, to think those modern English cognates or derivatives aid us in understanding the ancient Greek word as the original ancient speaker/writer would have. Think about the example given above. Dynamite is an explosive chemical concoction (originally called "Nobel's Blasting Powder"), invented by the Swedish chemist Alfred Nobel and patented in 1867. The apostle Paul was not thinking of dynamite when he penned Romans 1:16. Moreover, dynamite is often associated with destructive and potentially harmful explosions—not the associations Paul has in mind for the gospel in Romans 1:16.

In expositing James 1:21 ("Therefore, ridding yourselves of all moral filth and the evil that is so prevalent, humbly receive the implanted word, which is able to save your souls [ψυχάς]."), a famous (now deceased) preacher said:

> Well, you need to understand that salvation is in past tense, present tense, and future tense. In the past tense, we have been saved from the penalty of sin. In the present tense, our souls need to be saved from the power of sin day by day, right? We need to be delivered. Ah, one day, when Jesus comes, we're going to be saved from the very possibility of sin because we're going to be taken from the presence of sin and be made like the Lord Jesus Christ. Now it's that middle salvation that he's talking about—saving your soul from the power of sin. The Greek word for soul is what? Psyche or psuche. It's the same word, ah, we get, ah, psychiatric from, psychology from, psychic from. And what is the soul? Roughly speaking, it's, it's the mind, the emotion, the will. Now, when you receive the engrafted Word of God, it is able to deliver, to save, your mind, your emotion, and your will. That's what you need right now. You're already going to heaven, but what you need right now is that kind of salvation so you can live day by day as an overcomer.[13]

This preacher has not preached any heretical ideas, and his pastoral concerns are spot-on. Nevertheless, a more fundamental question is whether by employing ψυχάς (a form of ψυχή) in James 1:21, the inspired biblical author is intending to

---

[13] Adrian Rogers, *James*, Adrian Rogers Legacy Collection (audio transcript), accessed February 14, 2024, https://www.lwf.org/pdfs/20_James.pdf, 209.

describe the sanctifying influence of God's word on our minds, emotions, and will. Most commentators on the text recognize that "souls" here is a figure of speech known as *synecdoche*, in which a part represents the whole. (Here is an example of synecdoche: when a boat captain cries, "All hands on deck!" he expects more than severed hands to come to his aid. "Hands" represent the entire persons of the sailors.) In James 1:21, the soul represents the whole person. In other words, when James talks about people's souls being saved, he most likely refers to the final end-times deliverance of their whole person through the Day of Judgment. The New International Version captures this idea: "Therefore, get rid of all moral filth and the evil that is so prevalent and humbly accept the word planted in you, which can save you."

Perhaps it would be helpful to paste a few more reflections from my (Rob's) comments in the ESV Expositor's Bible Commentary on James:

> James declares that the divine word implanted in Christians is "able to save [their] souls." It is important to recognize that when New Testament authors use the verb [σῴζω] ("save") to refer to salvation (and not temporal healing), they usually are referring to a future deliverance from God's wrath at the final judgment (e.g., Rom 5:10). Modern, English-speaking evangelicals, on the other hand, frequently use the verb "save" to refer to one's initial regeneration or coming to faith. James here clearly has the future aspect of salvation in mind. By focusing on the power of the implanted divine Word to save them ultimately, James implicitly warns his audience against presumption. In other words, James calls these ancient Christians not to passivity and nominalism but to a believing and obedient response to the Christ-wrought act of God in their hearts. The teaching of the apostle Paul is similar: "For we are [God's] workmanship, created in Christ Jesus for good works, which God prepared beforehand, that we should walk in them" (Eph 2:10).[14]

---

[14] Robert L. Plummer, "James," in *Hebrews–Revelation*, ed. Iain M. Duguid, James M. Hamilton Jr., and Jay Sklar, ESV Expository Commentary, vol. 12 (Wheaton, IL: Crossway, 2018), 238–39 (the quote from Eph 2:10 is from the ESV).

2.3.3 Do Not Confuse Words and Concepts.

A diligent student of Scripture sometimes searches for every instance of a particular word in an effort to understand a theological concept. For example, a Christian seeking to understand prayer better may examine every instance of προσεύχομαι ("pray") in the NT. Such a student fails to consider, however, that the idea of prayer is mentioned in many places where the actual word προσεύχομαι is not used. In fact, the biblical authors employ many Greek words for prayer (e.g., δέησις, εὐχή, εὔχομαι), and the concept of prayer is sometimes present even when no explicit "prayer words" are used (John 11:41–42).

In a situation like this, you may wonder, "How can I discover what some of those other prayer-related words are so my search will be more comprehensive?" Great question! In chapter 4, we will learn about a lexical resource that groups words according to "semantic domain" (field of meaning) rather than in alphabetical order. So, for example, we would expect this resource to group all the words related to prayer together so you could, in turn, search for each of those words. Still, you need to remember that the concept of prayer/intercession can be present (in a parable, for example), where no explicit "prayer words" are used.

2.3.4 There Are No Exact Synonyms.

One of the worst tasks my children had in elementary school was an English writing assignment. The teacher required them to take a paragraph and look up a certain number of words in a thesaurus and then replace the current word in the given paragraph with a synonym from the thesaurus. (A thesaurus, theoretically, gives a list of synonyms for a word.) After my children did this exercise, the newly edited paragraph sounded ridiculous. The reality is there are no exact synonyms in a language. Yes, some words are very close. And, yes, some authors or speakers do use words synonymously *in particular contexts*, but there are other contexts where those words would not be synonymous. No words have the exact same range of meaning, nor do they fill the same "slot" in grammatical constructions. For example, what would you think if someone in your Sunday school class asked you to "strike the lights"? You would likely be surprised and confused. The speaker might reply, "Oh, my thesaurus says 'strike' and 'hit' mean the same thing." You would rightly respond (after reading this book, of course), "They overlap in range of meaning, but they are not synonymous. No words are exactly synonymous, and in the idiomatic expression you just used, only the word 'hit' works." ("Idiomatic" means the expression cannot be taken literally. It is a figure of speech.) If we are native English speakers, we all understand what it means to, "Hit the lights."

Many years ago, when I (Rob) was a seminary student, another student from Nigeria (Duro) was a dear friend of mine. He was excited that I was going to get married to Chandi, and he exclaimed, "Oh, Brother Rob, how wonderful that you will marry Chandi, and the two of you will have issue!" If you look up the word "issue" in a dictionary, perhaps the thirteenth definition will say, "biological offspring," which is clearly what Duro meant in his statement. He would have fulfilled well the thesaurus assignment that my children were given, but we all know that the word "issue" sounds strange and does not fit in this context.

The apostle John is well-known for having a particular style that uses *near* synonyms. Just yesterday, I had some students asking why John uses two different Greek adverbs in chapter 2 of his Gospel (v. 8, νῦν; v. 10, ἄρτι) that both translate as "now." The best answer is that John loves to vary his style with near synonyms, which are used here without any apparent difference in meaning. Also, the expression "until now" (ἕως ἄρτι) more commonly appears with ἄρτι. It probably just "sounded right" to ancient ears. John also uses ἀγαπάω ("love") and φιλέω ("love") interchangeably many times, but the words are not completely interchangeable because φιλέω can also mean "kiss" (as it does in Matt 26:48), but ἀγαπάω cannot mean "kiss."

2.4 POTENTIAL PERILS AFTER COMPLETING GREEK WORD STUDIES

There are not only perils before completing Greek word studies; there are also perils after completing them. Let us briefly consider some of the greatest dangers.

2.4.1 Don't Be Judgmental toward Persons Who Are Not Doing Word Studies as Responsibly as You.

As you grow in your understanding of Greek and how to responsibly do word studies, you will likely begin to notice errors in others. Perhaps an author or resource you once loved now strikes you as simplistic or flawed. Maybe even the preacher in your local church regularly commits linguistic fallacies that we have just covered in this chapter.

If you feel pride and judgmentalism sneaking into your heart, write out the following verse on an index card, memorize it, and prayerfully meditate on it. Ask God how it applies to the situation you are in:

> Therefore, as God's chosen ones, holy and dearly loved, put on compassion, kindness, humility, gentleness, and patience, bearing with one another and forgiving one another if anyone has a grievance against another. Just as the Lord has forgiven you, so you are also to forgive. Above all, put on love, which is the perfect bond of unity. (Col 3:12–14)

Seminary students sometimes ask me how they should deal with a pastor in their home church who uses Greek poorly. Most likely, you should say nothing. You should be glad, based on when and where he went to seminary, that he is a faithful Christian. You should pray for him. And when he asks you about the Greek in his sermon and what you thought about it, you can honestly say, "Sir, your sermon laid bare my sin. Thanks be to God." Because, in honesty, your sins of pride and judgmentalism were exposed by his preached word.[15]

2.4.2 Do Not Criticize English Bible Translations.

We have an embarrassing wealth of good English Bible translations. (See chapter 6 for further discussion of English Bible translations.) If you teach Sunday School and regularly say, "Wow, the ESV really butchers this verse here," or, "I can't believe the NIV got this one wrong again," what will the people under your tutelage conclude? They will potentially make the inferences that (1) the English Bibles they have are not reliable, and (2) there is little use in their reading the Bible on their own since they will likely not be able to discern the real meaning.

Causing people to distrust the Bible and not want to read it is bad spiritual fruit. Do not be a bearer of bad spiritual fruit.

---

[15] This paragraph was adapted from a faculty address I (Rob) gave at The Southern Baptist Theological Seminary, "The Necessity of Biblical Languages in Ministerial Training," September 2021.

2.4.3 Don't Be a Difficult Church Member.

As you grow in your knowledge of Greek word studies, ask yourself, "Am I building up the unity of my church, and am I supporting the church leadership?" As a seminary professor, I (Rob) regularly speak in churches around the country, and sometimes my former students (now pastors) confide in me over the difficult situations they are facing. One pastor recently told me about a church member who believed that the Yeti (Bigfoot) was real and came in and out of our space/time dimension through a worm hole! This pastor also confided in me about another church member who had become enamored with biblical word studies and was seeking to create a band of disciples around his particular interests. The church member did not realize how little he knew nor how divisive he was being. Knowledge, especially partial knowledge, can be dangerous. It can "puff us up" and make us proud (1 Cor 8:1), resulting in disunity and not the fruit of the Spirit. Pray the Lord uses your increased knowledge to form you into the image of Christ and to lovingly serve the church where God has placed you.

2.5 VOCABULARY

ἀδελφός	brother [and sister] (Philadelphia, the city of brotherly love)
ἄνθρωπος	man, human being, husband (anthropology, anthropomorphic)
εὐαγγέλιον	good news, gospel (evangelistic, evangelical)
θεός	God (theology)
κόσμος	world, universe; adornment (cosmos, cosmology, cosmetics)
κύριος	Lord, master, sir
λόγος	word, message, account (logic, theology, psychology)

2.6 PRACTICE EXERCISES[16]

A. **Exegetical Fallacies**: Label the following word study fallacies as illegitimate totality transfer, the etymological fallacy, or the reverse etymological fallacy.

[16] Videos featuring a textbook author working through the practice exercises are found at https://www.wordstudiesforeveryone.com. Before accessing those videos, you should

__________ A Bible teacher says, "Paul says here in 1 Thessalonians 1:6 that we are to become his imitators. The Greek word for imitator is μιμηταί. When I say, μιμηταί, you can hear that this is where we get the English word 'mimic.'"

__________ A Bible teacher says, "The Greek word here is τίθημι, which according to the lexicon, means, 'to put or place in a particular location, lay, put, explain, take off, give up, show deference to, place before someone, serve, have (in mind), effect something, arrange for something.'" (Note: these are actual definitions for τίθημι from a Greek lexicon. Some words have an especially wide range of meaning!)

__________ A Bible teacher says, "The Greek word here (ὑπηρέτης) is made up of two words (ὑπο + ἐρέτης)—one meaning "under" and the other meaning "rower," as attested in Homer's Greek (eighth century BC), so Paul here in 1 Corinthians 4:1 is saying we are to be "under rowers"—people on the lowest deck of the ship faithfully completing our menial service."

B. Writing: Practice handwriting and pronouncing your new Greek vocabulary words. Review your old words too. Write out the Greek alphabet from memory.

ἀδελφός __________________

ἄνθρωπος __________________

εὐαγγέλιον __________________

θεός __________________

κόσμος __________________

κύριος __________________

λόγος __________________

(1) study the material in this chapter and (2) attempt the activities without reference to the videos.

C. Reading: Practice reading aloud the following Greek text. Stress the accented syllables. Check yourself with the videos that accompany this textbook.

Philippians 1:1–11: Παῦλος καὶ Τιμόθεος δοῦλοι Χριστοῦ Ἰησοῦ πᾶσιν
τοῖς ἁγίοις ἐν Χριστῷ Ἰησοῦ τοῖς οὖσιν ἐν Φιλίπποις σὺν ἐπισκόποις
καὶ διακόνοις, 2 χάρις ὑμῖν καὶ εἰρήνη ἀπὸ θεοῦ πατρὸς ἡμῶν καὶ
κυρίου Ἰησοῦ Χριστοῦ. 3 Εὐχαριστῶ τῷ θεῷ μου ἐπὶ πάσῃ τῇ μνείᾳ ὑμῶν
4 πάντοτε ἐν πάσῃ δεήσει μου ὑπὲρ πάντων ὑμῶν, μετὰ χαρᾶς τὴν δέησιν
ποιούμενος, 5 ἐπὶ τῇ κοινωνίᾳ ὑμῶν εἰς τὸ εὐαγγέλιον ἀπὸ τῆς πρώτης
ἡμέρας ἄχρι τοῦ νῦν, 6 πεποιθὼς αὐτὸ τοῦτο, ὅτι ὁ ἐναρξάμενος ἐν ὑμῖν
ἔργον ἀγαθὸν ἐπιτελέσει ἄχρι ἡμέρας Χριστοῦ Ἰησοῦ· 7 Καθώς ἐστιν
δίκαιον ἐμοὶ τοῦτο φρονεῖν ὑπὲρ πάντων ὑμῶν διὰ τὸ ἔχειν με ἐν τῇ
καρδίᾳ ὑμᾶς, ἔν τε τοῖς δεσμοῖς μου καὶ ἐν τῇ ἀπολογίᾳ καὶ βεβαιώσει
τοῦ εὐαγγελίου συγκοινωνούς μου τῆς χάριτος πάντας ὑμᾶς ὄντας.
8 μάρτυς γάρ μου ὁ θεὸς ὡς ἐπιποθῶ πάντας ὑμᾶς ἐν σπλάγχνοις Χριστοῦ
Ἰησοῦ. 9 Καὶ τοῦτο προσεύχομαι, ἵνα ἡ ἀγάπη ὑμῶν ἔτι μᾶλλον καὶ
μᾶλλον περισσεύῃ ἐν ἐπιγνώσει καὶ πάσῃ αἰσθήσει 10 εἰς τὸ δοκιμάζειν
ὑμᾶς τὰ διαφέροντα, ἵνα ἦτε εἰλικρινεῖς καὶ ἀπρόσκοποι εἰς ἡμέραν
Χριστοῦ, 11 πεπληρωμένοι καρπὸν δικαιοσύνης τὸν διὰ Ἰησοῦ Χριστοῦ
εἰς δόξαν καὶ ἔπαινον θεοῦ.

CHAPTER 3

/////////////////

WHICH GREEK NEW TESTAMENT AM I READING? HOW CAN I BE SURE THESE ARE THE WORDS OF THE APOSTLES?

We recommend watching the video lecture before reading the chapter. The QR code and link to the video can be found on page x.

3.1 OVERVIEW

You are rightly hungering to do actual Greek word studies, but first we need to discuss the text of the GNT you will be reading. In other words, before you select a Greek word to study, you need to know you are selecting a word to study from the actual inspired writings of the apostles. Why are there versions of the GNT that differ in wording, and how can you be confident you are reading the actual Greek words which the Spirit-inspired apostles wrote? Even though you might not have thought to ask these foundational questions, soon you will understand the importance of addressing them.

3.2 SIGNIFICANCE

In John 21:15–17, when Jesus reinstates Peter, the verbs ἀγαπάω ("love") and φιλέω ("love") are central to the conversation. Many sermons have been preached claiming that properly understanding this passage turns on the nuanced difference between these two verbs—with Jesus asking if Peter loves him with a pure, divine love (ἀγαπάω), while Peter can only affirm a "friend-type" love (φιλέω). According to this understanding of the flow of the passage, Jesus ends with a piercing, "Peter, do you even love me like a friend (φιλέω)?" Jesus's conversation here certainly is piercing. (How would you like the Lord Jesus to ask you *three times* in succession, "Do you love me?"—especially after you had denied him *three times*?) But the assertion that the verb φιλέω means here "just a friend-type love" is likely wrong. We should probably see no difference in meaning here between ἀγαπάω and φιλέω. Modern English translations are correct to translate both words as "love." What are some arguments in favor of this view?

- In John 21:17, Peter was grieved because Jesus asked him "the third time" (note the explicit wording) whether he loved him. It is Jesus's repetition of the question, which implies some doubt about Peter's previous responses, which grieved the apostle.
- All writers and speakers have certain stylistic tendencies. The apostle John, for example, loves using nearly synonymous words with no intended different nuances of meaning. (See John 6:53–59, where John uses both the verbs ἐσθίω and τρώγω for eating.) In fact, John uses both verbs ἀγαπάω and φιλέω for the Father's love of the Son (e.g., John 3:35; 5:20). John's *idiolect* (i.e., his personal stylistic patterns) argues against seeing any intended semantic difference between the two verbs for "love" in John 21:15–17.
- During the Koine Greek period, the word φιλέω was used to mean both "love" (John 21:17) and kiss (Mark 14:44). It's understandable how a word with this range of meaning could cause confusion.[1] Does this potential confusion perhaps explain early Christians' statistically verifiable preference for the verb ἀγαπάω?
- It is sometimes wrongly asserted that ἀγαπάω can only refer to divine, self-giving love. God's love certainly is unique and self-giving, but we know that truth from the many descriptions of God's love in Scripture—not from the inherent semantic range (that is, the range of possible meanings) of the

[1] See Moisés Silva, *Biblical Words and Their Meaning: An Introduction to Lexical Semantics*, rev. ed. (Grand Rapids: Zondervan, 1994), 96.

word ἀγαπάω. In the ancient Greek translation of the OT (known as the *Septuagint* or referred to as LXX), 2 Samuel 13:15 uses the verb ἀγαπάω to describe Amnon's incestuous lust for his half-sister, Tamar.

3.3 UNDERSTANDING VARIOUS EDITIONS OF THE GREEK NEW TESTAMENT

If someone hands you a Greek New Testament (or directs you to an online or digital version), the first question you should ask is: "What text is this?" He or she might respond, "Well, it's the Greek New Testament, of course!" But, in actuality, there are many versions of the Greek New Testament, and you should be aware of the version you are reading. We will think more about text criticism (reconstructing the author's original wording from the ancient manuscripts we have) later in this chapter, but for now, you need to realize that all the original manuscripts of the New Testament have been lost. We do not have the Gospel of John written in the apostle's handwriting. Instead, we have copies of copies, and copies of copies of copies. We have thousands of ancient handwritten GNT manuscripts (or portions of manuscripts) stretching from the early second century up until the use of the printing press in the sixteenth century.

The majority of evangelical NT scholars believe that God has not preserved his Word in only one lineage of manuscripts. In other words, priority should not be given to manuscripts coming from a particular locale or tradition (e.g., preference to the Byzantine text tradition, as we find in the King James Only movement). It seems, rather, that God has preserved his Word through a multiplicity of ancient witnesses, traditions, and text families. Though these manuscripts agree in the majority of places, where they disagree, it is incumbent upon us to compare the manuscripts and consider their age, location, and the best explanation of the differences. That is, we seek to reconstruct the original apostolic wording through the practice of text criticism. As we compare these ancient manuscripts to put together a modern, edited compilation, the resulting text is called an "eclectic edition," because it is drawn from a variety of sources applying both internal and external criteria (see more on these criteria later in this chapter). Depending on one's presuppositions in practicing text criticism, a student can reach slightly different conclusions, which logically results in different preferences for which version of the GNT to use. Following are the main options:

- **Nestle-Aland, 28th edition** (also known as NA^{28}): The majority of NT scholars, whether evangelical or non-evangelical, consider the most recent Nestle-Aland (or United Bible Societies) edition of the GNT to be the most reliable. The text is overseen by an international committee of scholars from the *Institut für Neutestamentliche Textforschung* (INTF),[2] based in Münster, Germany. The actual Greek words of the Nestle-Aland edition and the United Bible Societies edition are the same, but they differ in some small ways—punctuation, formatting, and most significantly, the choice and presentation of textual variants (differing wording in ancient manuscripts). NA^{28} employs about a dozen "critical signs" (e.g., small circles, squares, squiggly lines, etc.) that are inserted within the Greek text and inform the reader of differences in the manuscript tradition. An apparatus at the bottom of the page gives more details. Significant variants that are contenders for the original wording are always included. But many noted variants are simply included as a matter of scholarly interest. The quantity and content of ancient manuscripts listed in the apparatus gives indication of whether a variant is significant or not, but the reader must have some familiarity with this material to assess it properly. At the time of this book's publication, the NA^{28} (first published in 2012) is the most recent NA edition, though a 29th edition is anticipated in the not-so-distant future. The 29th edition is expected to have revisions in Acts and Mark, as the detailed work of the *Editio Critica Maior* (see below) is gradually incorporated into the NA and UBS editions. The NA^{28} can be viewed free online (https://www.bibelwissenschaft.de/en/bible/NA28/), but the online version does not include either critical signs within the Greek text or the textual apparatus.
- **United Bible Societies, 5th edition**: Like the Nestle-Aland edition (see above), the text of the UBS^{5} is considered a scholarly standard, based on many decades of international committee work, with hundreds of years of NT textual study lying behind the more formal formation and oversight of the INTF. The main difference between the UBS and NA editions is the presentation of textual variants. The UBS edition focuses on variants that

[2] Also known by English speakers as the Institute for New Testament Textual Research, founded by Kurt Aland in 1959.

are either (a) more significant contenders for the original wording and/or (b) genuinely affect meaning and translation. As a result, far less variants are included in the textual apparatus at the bottom of the pages. Perhaps only one or two variants are listed per page, but a great amount of textual evidence is presented for these few variants. Also, variants are graded with a letter grade (i.e., A, B, C, or D) based on the editorial committee's certainty of reconstructing the original wording of the GNT. Though it needs to be updated, the *Textual Commentary on the Greek New Testament*, 2nd ed., by Bruce Metzger (based on the UBS^4), provides an invaluable discussion of the editorial committee's reasoning on every variant listed in the UBS. See also Roger L. Omanson's *A Textual Guide to the Greek New Testament* (Stuttgart: Deutsche Bibelgesellschaft, 2006).

- **Tyndale House Edition**: The Tyndale House evangelical study center at Cambridge University published an alternate eclectic critical text of the GNT in 2017.[3] A helpful introduction and defense of the edition appeared in 2019 as *An Introduction to the Greek New Testament Produced at Tyndale House, Cambridge*, by Dirk Jongkind (Crossway). The Tyndale House edition seeks to reflect some of the earliest features of extant ancient manuscripts, including unusual spellings, the dominant early order of NT books (i.e., placing the General Epistles before the Pauline epistles) and ancient methods of segmenting the text through *ekthesis* (extending the initial line of a paragraph into the margin, rather than indenting). The editors of the Tyndale House edition claim that the discovery of additional primary material (early papyri), improvements in the accuracy with which we can use early versions, and recent insights into scribal habits warrant a new critical edition of the GNT.[4] Every reading in the Tyndale House edition is represented by at least one Greek manuscript from the fifth century or earlier.[5] In an extensive blog post, Dirk Jongkind, the lead editor of this new edition, gives some sense of the differences between the Tyndale House and NA by comparing the book of Acts. He lists sixty-eight places

---

[3] See https://www.thegreeknewtestament.com.

[4] Wording from the Tyndale House edition website: https://www.thegreeknewtestament.com.

[5] A rule only violated in the book of Revelation.

where the texts differ.[6] I (Rob) tell my students that the Tyndale Greek New Testament is the *second* GNT they should buy (after purchasing the more widely accepted standard NA or UBS).[7]

- **Society of Biblical Literature (SBL) GNT**: Because it is freely available in digital format, many students use a SBL Greek New Testament for years without properly understanding its origin. The Society of Biblical Literature is a professional society of biblical scholars (of varied theological commitments), which has overseen the publication of this text (mainly in digital form). Michael Holmes, the editor of the SBL GNT, adjudicated between four previously published eclectic texts to arrive at the wording of his text,[8] which differs from the NA^{28}/UBS^{5} in about 540 places. At a practical level, the SBL GNT provides a close approximation to the NA/UBS text that can be legally distributed for free. Thus, for example, if you are viewing the GNT free online or in an app, you are probably viewing the SBL GNT. That is a good choice for most people using this book, but you should be aware of what you are using.
- **Zondervan ("Goodrich and Lukaszewski") GNT**: If you purchase a reader's edition (see below) of the GNT published by Zondervan, the Greek text you are reading is the one that "underlies the New International Version." In other words, the Committee on Bible Translation, which oversees the New International Version, made decisions about textual variants in the process of translation. Those cumulative decisions created, in essence, an underlying GNT, published in edited form by Richard J. Goodrich and Albert L. Lukaszewski. On a practical level, this underlying Greek text is very close to the NA/UBS text—allowing Zondervan to publish it without copyright violations. There are around 230 differences between the NA^{28}/UBS^{5} and the Zondervan ("Goodrich and Lukaszewski") GNT.
- **Robinson-Pierpont GNT**: Republished recently as *The New Testament in the Original Greek: Byzantine Textform 2018*, the Robinson-Pierpont

[6] Dirk Jongkind, "The Text of Acts—Differences between Tyndale House Edition, ECM, and NA28," *Evangelical Textual Criticism* (blog), August 29, 2018, http://evangelicaltextualcriticism.blogspot.com/2018/08/the-text-of-acts-differences-between.html.

[7] To view a twenty-minute video review of the Tyndale House edition by Rob Plummer, see https://vimeo.com/313496503.

[8] Westcott and Hort (WH), Tregelles (Treg), Goodrich and Lukaszewski (NIV), and Robinson and Pierpont (RP).

text provides a critical edition of the Byzantine textform. A small minority of scholars believe the Byzantine text tradition provides the most reliable transmission of the GNT manuscripts, and a defense of that view by Maurice Robinson can be read free online.[9] The Byzantine text tradition underlies the King James Version, so a commitment to Byzantine text priority is usually part of the "King James Only" movement. Nevertheless, not every scholar favoring the Byzantine text tradition is a proponent of King James-onlyism. For an irenic response to KJV-only claims, see James R. White, *The King James Only Controversy: Can You Trust the Modern Translations?* Rev. ed. (Minneapolis: Bethany House, 2009).

- ***Editio Critica Maior***: The *Editio Critica Maior* (*ECM*) is an ongoing, multi-volume critical scholarly edition of the GNT. Because of the detail and price of this work, you will likely only view it in a library. The ECM provides a comprehensive, computer-based analysis of all significant text variations within the first thousand years of the GNT's transmission and is overseen by the INTF. The INTF is gradually incorporating the published decisions of the *ECM* into new revisions of the NA/UBS. The NA^{28}/UBS^{5}, for example, reflects the *ECM* text of the General Epistles (James-Jude), differing in thirty-four places from the NA^{27}/UBS^{4}. The NA^{29}/UBS^{6} (forthcoming) is expected to incorporate *ECM*-based revisions in the book of Acts and the Gospel of Mark.[10] The entire *ECM* project is slated to be completed by 2030, but at its current pace, we would label that timeline "aspirational."
- **Other Editions**: By now, you are likely very curious as to which version of the GNT you have been viewing online. Go down that rabbit hole into the lesser-visited pages of your chosen GNT website/app and see if you can figure it out. If the Greek text is not one of the editions listed above, it is likely an earlier critical edition that is now in the public domain and thus can be distributed freely online. For example, it's not uncommon to find the "Westcott-Hort" text, an earlier "Nestle" edition, or a version edited by "Tregelles," which would all fit within the category of earlier critical editions now in the public domain. Should you be worried about this? No.

---

[9] See Maurice A. Robinson, "New Testament Textual Criticism: The Case for Byzantine Priority," *TC: A Journal of Biblical Textual Criticism* (2001), http://www.reltech.org/TC/v06/Robinson2001.html.

[10] There are fifty-two differences between the *ECM* and the NA^{28} in the book of Acts.

> Though there are many minor differences in ancient manuscripts and critical editions, you will likely not notice them. At the same time, we have presented above the consensus of good scholarship, so it's desirable to have the most accurate edition of the GNT.

In addition to deciding which Greek text to use online or purchase in print edition, one must make a decision about formatting. The main choices are (1) regular text, (2) reader's edition, and (3) interlinear. For most people reading this book, an interlinear is probably the best choice. An interlinear text puts the Greek text directly above (or below) the English translation, so you can easily follow along and see which Greek words lie behind the English. For a printed Greek-English interlinear text, we recommend the *Greek-English Interlinear CSB New Testament* (Nashville: Bible Holman Publishers, 2022). This interlinear is revolutionary in providing a windowed reading card that can be used to cover up the English line of text. As the students grow in their skill of reading, less assistance can be used. Furthermore, the vocabulary notes at the bottom of the page enable this interlinear to function like a reader's edition (see below for more on reader's editions). For a free online Greek interlinear text, we recommend: https://biblehub.com/interlinear/.

Although most readers of this book will not be ready for a GNT reader's edition or regular edition, we will briefly introduce them. A reader's edition provides English definitions of rare vocabulary words at the bottom of the page. Depending on the formatting of the chosen reader's edition, assistance for rare or difficult grammatical forms is sometimes provided too. Even students who have studied Greek for years can be discouraged if they are constantly having to stop and look up rare vocabulary or stumbling over strange constructions. A reader's edition is a great choice for the intermediate Greek student and pastor.

A regular text GNT edition can also be a good option for advanced students—usually providing more extensive text-critical information, supplementary apparatuses, and introductory essays (in comparison with a reader's version). If you buy a regular text version of the GNT and are struggling with rare vocabulary, you can always use a digital resource (such as https://app.biblearc.com) for vocabulary assistance or access a separately published reader's lexicon to help speed you along.[11]

---

[11] We recommend: Michael H. Burer and Jeffrey E. Miller, *A New Reader's Lexicon of the Greek New Testament* (Grand Rapids: Kregel, 2008). This resource provides rare vocabulary of the GNT, verse by verse, in canonical order.

Never in the history of the world has there been less need to purchase a printed GNT. There are many excellent and free options to read the GNT from your smartphone, tablet, or computer. At the same time, never has it been easier or cheaper to acquire a printed GNT. And there are many reasons to buy one—not least, the joy of reading the biblical text without the constant temptation to digital distraction. (Are we the only ones tempted to check the weather or news headlines?)[12]

3.4 CAN I BE CONFIDENT THAT I AM READING THE WORDS OF THE APOSTLES?

Every curious Christian must at some point ask, "How can I be confident that the Bible I am reading has been faithfully preserved from the days of the prophets and apostles?" Some popular movies, books, and radio-show pundits raise this question with intense skepticism.

As the book in your hands pertains to New Testament Greek, we are going to narrow that original question a bit more: "How can you be confident that the words in your modern GNT (whether in printed or digital format) are a faithful transmission of the authors' originally penned words?" This is a legitimate question, and it is the question answered by the field of *text criticism*.

A detailed introduction to text criticism is beyond the scope of this book, but in the next few pages, we hope to overview the topic and point you in the direction of resources for more extensive discussion.[13]

We do not have the original copies (autographs) of the NT documents. Yet, even within the NT itself, we have evidence that the individual NT documents were copied by hand and that these copies circulated among the churches. In Colossians 4:16, Paul writes, "After this letter has been read at your gathering, have it read also in the church of the Laodiceans; and see that you also read the

[12] Also, most people find that their memory of reading a printed GNT includes an added spatial dimension. In other words, you may remember where on the physical page you read certain phrases, and as you flip back through your printed GNT, your memory of the placement of those words on the page helps you locate the passage and further reinforces your memory.

[13] Several of the paragraphs below are adapted from Andreas J. Köstenberger, Benjamin L. Merkle, and Robert L. Plummer, *Going Deeper with New Testament Greek: An Intermediate Study of the Grammar and Syntax of the New Testament*, rev. ed. (Nashville: B&H Academic, 2020), 24–32.

letter from Laodicea."[14] Over time, the early church grouped selections of inspired writings and copied them together. By the mid-second century, the four canonical Gospels and Paul's letters were apparently grouped and copied as units. Not much later, the entire NT was grouped and copied as a recognized body of inspired writings. The earliest extant canonical list we have of the NT (the Muratorian Canon) has been dated to AD 190.[15] As early Christians copied, recopied, and copied copies (all by hand), small variations were inevitably introduced into the manuscripts. And, although Church Fathers sometimes speculated about copyist errors or the original reading of manuscripts,[16] it was virtually impossible to codify accurately such discussion until one could reproduce a text without any variation. Thus, after the printing press was introduced to Europe in 1454, possibilities for comparing manuscripts with an unchanging standard arose. At roughly the same time, Europe experienced a revival of interest in classical learning (including the Greek language) and the arrival of the Protestant Reformation (where focus on the meaning of the inspired Scripture necessitated careful argumentation from the text of Scripture in the original languages). The printing press, a revived knowledge of Greek, and a growing interest in the gospel combined to result in the first published printed edition of the GNT by Erasmus in 1516.[17] In producing this text, Erasmus relied on only seven manuscripts, most of poor quality.[18] Today, we have more than

---

[14] Some scholars have suggested that this "letter from Laodicea" may be Paul's canonical letter to the Ephesians, as the words ἐν Ἐφέσῳ ("in Ephesus," Eph 1:1) are lacking in significant ancient manuscripts.

[15] The Muratorian canon is dated by some scholars as late as the fourth century. For a brief presentation of the views, see Edmon L. Gallagher and John D. Meade, *The Biblical Canon Lists from Early Christianity: Texts and Analysis* (Oxford: Oxford University Press, 2017), 174–83. Certainly, however, Christians distinguished canonical from non-canonical writings before the earliest extant canonical lists, as evidenced by both the NT (e.g., 2 Thess 2:2; 3:17) and the writings of the Apostolic Fathers.

[16] For example, Jerome, Augustine, and Origen. See Bruce M. Metzger and Bart D. Ehrman, *The Text of the New Testament: Its Transmission, Corruption, and Restoration*, 4th ed. (New York: Oxford University Press, 2005), 200–203.

[17] The Complutensian Polyglot, a printed GNT produced under the direction of Cardinal Ximenes, was apparently completed in 1514 but not formally published until after Erasmus's text.

[18] See Edwin M. Yamauchi, "Erasmus' Contributions to New Testament Scholarship," *Fides et Historia* 19, no. 3 (1987): 10–11. Yamauchi writes, "Although Erasmus claimed that he used 'the oldest and most correct copies of the New Testament,' the press of the

5,000 ancient manuscripts (or partial manuscripts) of the GNT, with the number increasing yearly.[19]

Subsequent generations continued to build on the foundational work of Erasmus in producing "standard" printed versions of the GNT derived from the various ancient manuscripts available to them. Until the mid-nineteenth century, the Byzantine text tradition was assumed as the standard.[20] It was sometimes called the *Textus Receptus* (received text), so labeled in the preface to a GNT published by the Elzevir brothers in 1633. Over time, principles for adjudicating disputed readings were developed and accepted by the majority of scholars.[21] The Byzantine text came to be viewed by many as a later conflation of text traditions and lost its primacy to "eclectic" scholarly editions produced by text critics. Principles that dethroned the Byzantine text and codified the modern discipline of text criticism can be traced to the seminal work of Brian Walton (1600–1661), Johann Bengel (1687–1752), Karl Lachmann (1793–1851), Constantine von Tischendorf (1815–1874), B. F. Westcott (1825–1901), F. J. A. Hort (1828–1892), and others.

It should be noted that a small minority of scholars insist that only one "family" of ancient manuscripts (the Byzantine family) preserves the most reliable text of the NT. Yet, even within this Byzantine family of manuscripts, there are numerous minor variations. Modern English-speaking persons who insist on the priority of the Byzantine text family are often aligned in some way with the King James Only movement. They argue that the King James Version (the NT of which is translated from a Byzantine version of the Greek text) is the

---

publisher's deadline forced him to rely on but seven rather late and inferior manuscripts available at Basle" (10).

[19] Daniel Wallace, director of the Center for the Study of New Testament Manuscripts (CSNTM), regularly reports the discovery of new and significant ancient manuscripts on the center's website, http://www.csntm.org.

[20] Scholars also speak of the "Majority text," which means the reading found in the majority of extant NT manuscripts. As the majority of extant NT manuscripts are Byzantine, these terms overlap. Most Byzantine text readings are considered, by pure mathematical reckoning, as "the Majority text." Of course, because nearly all NT text traditions overlap at roughly 90 percent, any NT text will be representative of "the Majority text" at most points.

[21] See Eldon Jay Epp's critique of these traditional text-critical principles in "Traditional 'Canons' of New Testament Textual Criticism: Their Value, Validity, and Viability—or Lack Thereof," in *The Textual History of the Greek New Testament: Changing Views in Contemporary Research*, Text Critical Studies 8, ed. Klaus Wachtel and Michael W. Holmes (Atlanta: SBL, 2011), 79–127.

most reliable because it is based on the best-preserved manuscript tradition. The majority of evangelical Christian scholars, however, believe the evidence points to God preserving his Word through the multiplicity of manuscripts in a variety of text families. God has left us so many manuscripts of such high quality that, even in the places where there are variants in the manuscripts, we can reach a high level of certainty as to what the original text read.[22] God has not seen fit to preserve the *autographs* (apostolically-penned originals) of the NT, but he has preserved *all the words of the autographs* in the many manuscripts that have come down to us.

Traditionally, the discipline of text criticism has sought to determine the original wording of an ancient text whose autograph has disappeared and whose existing manuscripts exhibit variations. The criteria for determining the original reading of the text can be divided into external and internal criteria. External criteria concern the age, quantity, and provenance (i.e., geographical origin) of the manuscripts consulted. Internal criteria consider scribal tendencies, as well as how a disputed variant fits within the context of the document (the author's style or the context of his argument). Some prominent modern text critics are known for strongly favoring external or internal criteria, but a reasoned use of all available criteria seems judicious. As scholars consider manuscript variants, they are like detectives—using their knowledge of the manuscript they are studying along with their understanding of common scribal mistakes or tendencies to both reconstruct the original text and explain variant readings.

The GNT that results from deciding among disputed readings is called an *eclectic text*. The word "eclectic" means "drawn from a variety of sources." In labeling our final product as an "eclectic" text, we are recognizing that there is no ancient manuscript that parallels it word-for-word. While our eclectic GNT overlaps overwhelmingly with the vast majority of all ancient GNT manuscripts, it is, in the end, drawn from a multiplicity of sources, not agreeing at every point with any of them. Academically respected texts (like the NA^{28} edition of the GNT) are often called "critical texts" not because they are critical of anything but because

---

[22] For an essay defending the reliability of the GNT, see Daniel B. Wallace, "Has the New Testament Text Been Hopelessly Corrupted?," in *In Defense of the Bible: A Comprehensive Apologetic for the Authority of Scripture*, ed. Steven B. Cowan and Terry L. Wilder (Nashville: B&H, 2013), 139–63.

they have been carefully and painstakingly compiled by the best-known scholarly methods.

Changes by ancient scribes to the exemplars they were copying can be loosely classified as unintentional errors versus intentional changes. We will briefly look at examples of both:

3.4.1 Unintentional Errors[23]

1. *Errors of Sight*. Scribes sometimes copied texts by looking back and forth to a manuscript. By this method, they inevitably made a number of errors of sight. For example, they confused letters that looked similar in appearance, divided words wrongly (the oldest Greek manuscripts of the Bible have no spaces between words), repeated words or sections (i.e., copied the same thing twice), accidentally skipped letters, words or sections, or changed the order of letters in a word or words in a sentence. In Codex Vaticanus, for example, at Galatians 1:11, a scribe accidentally wrote τὸ εὐαγγέλιον ("the gospel") three times in succession.
2. *Errors of Hearing*. When scribes copied manuscripts through dictation (i.e., scribes wrote as a manuscript was being read aloud) errors of hearing were made. For example, vowels, diphthongs, or other sounds were misheard, as in Matthew 2:6 in Codex Sinaiticus, where ἐκ σοῦ ("from you") has been wrongly heard and written as ἐξ οὗ ("from whom"). We make similar mistakes in English, for instance, writing "night" when someone says, "knight."
3. *Errors of Writing*. Sometimes scribes introduced errors simply by writing the wrong thing. For example, a scribe might accidentally add an additional letter to the end of a word—resulting in a different meaning. In Codex Alexandrinus, at John 13:37, a scribe accidentally wrote δύνασαί

[23] The material below is from Robert L. Plummer, *40 Questions About Interpreting the Bible*, 2nd ed. (Grand Rapids: Kregel, 2021), 60–63, originally derived from Arthur G. Patzia, *The Making of the New Testament: Origin, Collection, Text & Canon*, 2nd ed. (Downers Grove, IL: InterVarsity, 2011), 230–42.

μοι rather than δύναμαί σοι. Rather than saying to Jesus, "Why can't I follow you now?" Peter queries, "Why can't you follow me now?"[24]

4. *Errors of Judgment*. Sometimes scribes exercised poor judgment by incorporating marginal glosses (ancient footnotes) into the body of the text or by other egregious copying misjudgments. In the fourteenth-century Codex 109, for example, a scribe has apparently copied continuous lines of text from a manuscript that listed the genealogy of Jesus (Luke 3:23–38) in two columns. The resulting genealogy has all the family relations scrambled, even listing God as the son of Aram.[25]

3.4.2 Intentional Errors

A minority of textual variants resulted from intentional activity on the part of scribes. Such changes included:

1. *Revising Grammar and Spelling*. In an attempt to standardize grammar or spelling, scribes sometimes corrected what they perceived as orthographic or grammatical errors in the text they were copying. For example, though John originally put the nominative case (ὁ ὤν) after the *preposition* ἀπό in Revelation 1:4, later scribes have inserted a genitive form (θεοῦ).[26]
2. *Harmonizing Similar Passages*. Scribes had a tendency to harmonize parallel passages and introduce uniformity to stylized expressions. For example, details from the same incident in multiple Gospels might be included when copying any one Gospel. As professors of Greek, we have found it interesting that students sometimes unintentionally insert "Lord" or "Christ" when translating a passage with the name "Jesus." Normally, such students are not intending to promote a "higher Christology;" they are simply conforming their speech to a stylized reference to the Savior. Ancient scribes behaved in a similar way.
3. *Eliminating Apparent Discrepancies and Difficulties*. Scribes sometimes "fixed" what they perceived as a problem in the text. Metzger and Ehrman

[24] This variant is also possibly an "error of sight" (i.e., the scribe's eyes jumped to the parallel expression in John 13:36). We are indebted to Elijah Hixson for pointing out this variant, as well as some other variants mentioned in this section.

[25] Metzger and Ehrman, *The Text of the New Testament*, 259.

[26] Metzger and Ehrman, 262.

report that because Origen perceived a geographical difficulty at John 1:28, he changed Βηθανίᾳ ("Bethany") to Βηθαβαρᾶ ("Bethabara").[27]

4. *Conflating the Text.* Sometimes when a scribe knew of variant readings in the manuscript base from which he was copying, he would simply include both variants within his copy. For example, in Acts 20:28, some early manuscripts read τὴν ἐκκλησίαν τοῦ θεοῦ ("the church of God"), while others read τὴν ἐκκλησίαν τοῦ κυρίου ("church of the Lord"). Later manuscripts conflate the readings as τὴν ἐκκλησίαν τοῦ κυρίου καὶ [τοῦ] θεοῦ ("the church of the Lord and God").[28]
5. *Adapting Different Liturgical Traditions.* In a few isolated places, it is possible that church liturgy (i.e., stylized prayers or praises) influenced some textual additions or wording changes (e.g., Matthew 6:13, "For yours is the kingdom, and the power, and the glory forever. Amen.").
6. *Making Theological or Doctrinal Changes.* Sometimes scribes made theological or doctrinal changes—either omitting something they saw as wrong or making clarifying additions. For example, in Matthew 24:36, some manuscripts omit the reference to the Son's ignorance of the day of his return—a passage that is obviously difficult to understand.[29]

In recent decades, the field of NT textual criticism has experienced a revival of interest. The digitization of most significant ancient GNT manuscripts has democratized access to primary materials. (View, for example, the entire Codex Sinaiticus in stunning clarity at http://www.codexsinaiticus.org). Computers have also changed the traditional and overly simplistic categorization of manuscripts into broad text families. Computer algorithms are helping sort out complex genealogical relationships between ancient manuscripts and are at the heart of the ongoing revision of the standard critical editions of the GNT (i.e., the *Editio Critica Maior*, the Nestle-Aland, and the United Bible Societies editions). Also, there has been a flowering of interest in scribal tendencies and what they reveal about the

---

[27] Metzger and Ehrman, 264.

[28] Metzger and Ehrman, 265.

[29] In this text, as in a few other places (e.g., John 4:6), Scripture seems to speak of Jesus from the perspective of his human nature, not intending to deny the omniscience or omnipotence of his divine nature. Others have explained this passage by claiming that before his exaltation, Jesus emptied himself of certain divine prerogatives (i.e., the kenotic theory).

theological predilections of ancient scribes and the communities they represent. There has never been a more exciting time to explore the field of text criticism.

3.5 RESOURCES FOR FURTHER STUDY OF NT TEXTUAL CRITICISM

- Charles L. Quarles and L. Scott Kellem. *40 Questions about the Text and Canon of the New Testament*. 40 Questions Series. Grand Rapids: Kregel, 2023.
- Elijah Hixson and Peter J. Gurry, eds. *Myths and Mistakes in New Testament Textual Criticism*. Downers Grove: IVP Academic, 2019. This is a recent and engaging book edited by two text critical scholars.
- https://evangelicaltextualcriticism.blogspot.com/. This blog provides an evangelical window into current text critical discussions.
- https://podcasts.apple.com/us/podcast/the-basics-of-new-testament-textual-criticism/id446655163. Via this free podcast, you can view fifteen foundational lectures on NT text criticism by evangelical text critic Dan Wallace.
- https://www.credocourses.com/product/textual-criticism/. This text criticism class, also by Dan Wallace, is more extensive than the free podcast videos (see above). The class and accompanying resources are available for purchase from the apologetics ministry Credo House.
- www.csntm.org. The Center for the Study of New Testament Manuscripts (CSNTM) is a non-profit ministry led by Dan Wallace that focuses on digitizing manuscripts of the GNT.
- https://newtestamentgreekportal.blogspot.com/p/textual-criticism.html. Southeastern Seminary's David Alan Black's "text criticism" section of his NT Greek Portal provides summaries of text critical resources and helpful links.

3.6 VOCABULARY

(In Greek lexicons, it is normal to list the first-person singular form of the *verb* as the dictionary form—thus the form of the definitions below.)

ἀκούω	I hear, listen to, obey (acoustics)
γινώσκω	I know, understand, acknowledge (knowledge, Gnostics)

γράφω	I write (graphics)
εἰμί	I am, exist
ἔρχομαι	I come, go
πιστεύω	I believe, have faith/trust in
ἀλλά[30]	but, yet, nevertheless

3.7 PRACTICE EXERCISES[31]

A. Writing: Practice handwriting and pronouncing your new Greek vocabulary words. Review your old words too. Write out the Greek alphabet from memory.

ἀκούω ____________________
γινώσκω ____________________
γράφω ____________________
εἰμί ____________________
ἔρχομαι ____________________
πιστεύω ____________________
ἀλλά ____________________

B. Online Greek NT: Spend at least 20 minutes exploring the three free online versions of the Greek New Testament listed below. How are they different? List significant details you noticed about them.

- https://app.biblearc.com
- https://www.greekbible.com
- https://biblehub.com/interlinear/

---

[30] The final vowel of ἀλλά is often dropped when the next word begins with a vowel (ἀλλ').

[31] Videos featuring a textbook author working through the practice exercises are found at https://www.wordstudiesforeveryone.com. Before accessing them, you should (1) study the material in this chapter and (2) attempt the activities without reference to the videos.

C. **Printed Greek NT**: Write a one paragraph essay explaining which printed edition of the GNT you are going to buy and why. (Or, perhaps explain why you are not going to buy a printed GNT at this time.) Provide an online link to your preferred edition. Compare and contrast the version you plan to buy with other versions of the GNT. Why did you decide on this one?

D. **Textual Criticism**: Spend at least 20 minutes exploring the online text criticism resources above. Write one paragraph summarizing what you learned in your foray into the world of NT textual criticism. Does NT textual criticism interest you enough to study further on your own? If so, make a plan of specific "next steps."

E. **Reading**: Practice reading aloud the following Greek text. Stress the accented syllables. Check yourself with the videos that accompany this textbook.

James 1:1–12: Ἰάκωβος θεοῦ καὶ κυρίου Ἰησοῦ Χριστοῦ δοῦλος
ταῖς δώδεκα φυλαῖς ταῖς ἐν τῇ διασπορᾷ χαίρειν. 2 Πᾶσαν χαρὰν
ἡγήσασθε, ἀδελφοί μου, ὅταν πειρασμοῖς περιπέσητε ποικίλοις,
3 γινώσκοντες ὅτι τὸ δοκίμιον ὑμῶν τῆς πίστεως κατεργάζεται
ὑπομονήν. 4 ἡ δὲ ὑπομονὴ ἔργον τέλειον ἐχέτω, ἵνα ἦτε τέλειοι καὶ
ὁλόκληροι ἐν μηδενὶ λειπόμενοι. 5 Εἰ δέ τις ὑμῶν λείπεται σοφίας,
αἰτείτω παρὰ τοῦ διδόντος θεοῦ πᾶσιν ἁπλῶς καὶ μὴ ὀνειδίζοντος,
καὶ δοθήσεται αὐτῷ. 6 αἰτείτω δὲ ἐν πίστει μηδὲν διακρινόμενος·
ὁ γὰρ διακρινόμενος ἔοικεν κλύδωνι θαλάσσης ἀνεμιζομένῳ καὶ
ῥιπιζομένῳ. 7 μὴ γὰρ οἰέσθω ὁ ἄνθρωπος ἐκεῖνος ὅτι λήμψεταί τι
παρὰ τοῦ κυρίου, 8 ἀνὴρ δίψυχος, ἀκατάστατος ἐν πάσαις ταῖς
ὁδοῖς αὐτοῦ. 9 Καυχάσθω δὲ ὁ ἀδελφὸς ὁ ταπεινὸς ἐν τῷ ὕψει
αὐτοῦ, 10 ὁ δὲ πλούσιος ἐν τῇ ταπεινώσει αὐτοῦ, ὅτι ὡς ἄνθος
χόρτου παρελεύσεται. 11 ἀνέτειλεν γὰρ ὁ ἥλιος σὺν τῷ καύσωνι
καὶ ἐξήρανεν τὸν χόρτον, καὶ τὸ ἄνθος αὐτοῦ ἐξέπεσεν, καὶ ἡ
εὐπρέπεια τοῦ προσώπου αὐτοῦ ἀπώλετο· οὕτως καὶ ὁ πλούσιος ἐν
ταῖς πορείαις αὐτοῦ μαρανθήσεται. 12 Μακάριος ἀνὴρ ὃς ὑπομένει
πειρασμόν, ὅτι δόκιμος γενόμενος λήμψεται τὸν στέφανον τῆς ζωῆς
ὃν ἐπηγγείλατο τοῖς ἀγαπῶσιν αὐτόν.

CHAPTER 4

////////////////

GREEK WORD STUDY RESOURCES

We recommend watching the video lecture before reading the chapter. The QR code and link to the video can be found on page x.

4.1 OVERVIEW

We have finally arrived. It is time to introduce you to some actual Greek word study resources and how to use them. Perhaps you didn't notice, but we've been gradually building your skill in reading and writing Greek words. This purposeful journey has led us to the place where you are ready to use a Greek lexicon. Don't be overwhelmed by the more advanced resources we also introduce in this chapter. Studying the GNT is a lifelong mission, and though you can benefit from any knowledge of Greek, there is always more to learn, even for the most advanced student.

4.2 SIGNIFICANCE

In English, "this/these" and "that/those" are *demonstrative pronouns*. The Greek language also has demonstrative pronouns. Ancient writers could employ demonstrative pronouns for a variety of reasons. The apostle John seems to use them as a matter of personal style, with many of his demonstrative pronouns seeming interchangeable with personal pronouns. Such demonstratives are usually translated into modern English Bibles as personal pronouns.[1] Otherwise, a modern English reader would be jarred by the unusual frequency of "this one," "that one," "those ones" in the translation without apparent contrast or emphasis indicated by the broader context.

Another reason an ancient author employed demonstrative pronouns was for rhetorical emphasis or contrast. We use such pronouns the same way in English: "Don't be like *that* man." The word "that" here has a disparaging function by implicitly contrasting "that" man with other men, who are apparently not as bad as he.

In James 1:7, James writes, "*That* person should not expect to receive anything from the Lord" (NIV, emphasis added). Even without further context, we can detect the heightened emphasis and contrast that comes from employing the *demonstrative pronoun* "that" (ἐκεῖνος in Greek). What exactly is wrong with *that* man such that he should not think he will receive anything from the Lord? James tells us that man has not brought his petitions to God in faith, but rather with doubting (1:6). In the surrounding verses, James describes the doubting petitioner with some colorful images—he is like a blown and tossed sea wave (v. 6), double-minded and unstable in all his ways (v. 8).

James's teaching echoes several places in Jesus's earthly ministry in which the Lord demanded faith of those who came to him. In Matthew 9:29, as Jesus touched the blind men's eyes, he said, "According to your faith be it done to you" (ESV). To the demon-possessed child's father, who was wavering in unbelief, Jesus said, "All things are possible for one who believes" (Mark 9:23 ESV). When Jesus was asked by his disciples why they could not cast out an evil spirit, he responded, "Because of your little faith. . . . For truly I tell you, if you have faith the size of a mustard seed, you will tell this mountain, 'Move from here to there,' and it will move. Nothing will be impossible for you" (Matt 17:20). Likewise, the author of Hebrews warns, "Without faith it is impossible to please God, since the one who draws near to him must believe that he exists and that he rewards those who seek him" (Heb 11:6).

When James calls for faith, he is not calling for Christians to work up some sort of invisible faith-o-meter so they "feel" their prayer is being answered in an overly specific way. Rather, Christians are to approach God trustingly—knowing he is powerful, good, and kindly disposed to them because of the relationship

---

[1] E.g., John 13:25, ἐκεῖνος, "that one," translated as "he."

secured through Christ's perfect life and atoning death. The opposite of such faith is to think God does not really care, is not good, and does not keep his fatherly promises in Christ.

Sensitive Christians can sometimes fret a great deal over whether they have enough faith. In James's strong words about doubt, he is not addressing such sensitive believers. Rather, James is rebuking the presumptuous and erratic petitioner who seeks to live independent of God at one moment, but offers up a quick, unbelieving plea when desperation or inclination strikes. That person cannot expect to receive anything from God.[2]

4.3 GREEK WORD STUDY RESOURCES YOU SHOULD NOT USE

In the original plan for this book (i.e., in a proposal submitted to the publisher), we envisioned a chapter entitled, "Word Study Tools Can Be Dangerous!" We explained, "This chapter looks at some popular resources and why they are not recommended." Upon further reflection, we decided to exercise greater Christian charity and reduce this chapter to a brief sub-section of another chapter. We could have hundreds of conversations with readers of this book about this topic, so insert yourself into the dialogue below that best fits you:

Dialogue #1

You: Hey, my uncle was a pastor and gave me this set of word study books by _____. Are those any good?

Us: Well, they have some value, but we don't consider them the best, so we didn't recommend them.

You: Should I use them?

Us: If you could drive a new Porche, why would you drive a rusty Toyota Tercel?

You: But, my uncle—

Us: OK, now. That's enough of that.

[2] A portion of this section was adapted from Robert L. Plummer, "James" in *Hebrews–Revelation*, ed. Iain M. Duguid, James M. Hamilton Jr., and Jay Sklar, ESV Expository Commentary, vol. 12 (Wheaton, IL: Crossway, 2018), 230–32.

Dialogue #2

You: Hey, you didn't include my favorite word study resource that I own—the one by _____.

Us: That's right. We didn't. Although it has some value, and we don't doubt the devotion of the person who created it, there are better resources out there.

Dialogue #3

You: I can't believe you didn't include Strong's Concordance. It's a classic.

Us: Strong's Concordance is for people who can't read Greek. That's why it has all those numbers, so you can flip around and try to figure out what Greek words underlie the English words you are looking up.

You: Oh.

Us: You see, we are calling you to a higher level—to actually learn to read Greek words so you can use the best resources available.

You: I see. Thanks for believing in me, guys!

Us: *(two thumbs up from authors)*

4.4 GREEK WORD STUDY RESOURCES YOU SHOULD USE

For most readers of this book, two Greek word study resources will suffice to give you "the best of the best." Are they cheap? No. But, they probably cost less than you regularly spend on your hobbies. Furthermore, you can ask pastors at your church to acquire these items to be put on reserve in your church library. The two resources we are recommending are (1) a lexicon and (2) a theological dictionary set.

4.4.1 The Lexicon We Recommend

"Lexicon" is just another word for a dictionary. Whether in print or digital format, a Greek-English lexicon is needed by every serious student of the GNT. At first, you will likely access Thayer's classic lexicon for free via an online GNT or the

Internet Archive.[3] There comes a point, however, where you rightly desire the best NT Greek lexicon available. It is:

> Danker, Frederick William, rev. and ed. *A Greek-English Lexicon of the New Testament and Other Early Christian Literature*, 3rd ed. Chicago: University of Chicago Press, 2000.

Please note that this is a Greek lexicon specifically focused on the time period and vocabulary of the Greek New Testament and other early Christian literature. This lexicon is universally referred to as "BDAG" (spoken as two syllables: Bee-Dag). The "D" in BDAG stands for Frederick Danker (1920–2012). Danker's updates to this third edition have made this resource much more user-friendly. The second edition of this text (1979) was known as BAGD because of key scholars who had contributed to it (Walter <u>B</u>auer, William F. <u>A</u>rndt, F. Wilbur <u>G</u>ingrich, and Frederick W. <u>D</u>anker). In the shorthand title for the third edition of this text (BDAG), Danker's name is now listed second to Bauer, who compiled the German lexicon upon which later editions were based. Though BDAG is expensive, you will want to have a copy—either in digital or print format.

You may be tempted to save a great deal of money by buying the 1979 second edition (BAGD) of this lexicon off eBay. When I (Rob) have students tempted to do that, I tell them to go to our seminary's library, put the second and third edition next to each other, and open to an entry for the same word. I instruct them to compare the entries and see if they would be happy with the second edition. Frankly, though the second edition contains much helpful information, the formatting makes the volume virtually unusable to the average reader. So, if you are still tempted to buy the second edition, perhaps you should try my suggested exercise. I'm confident that you will be deterred.

There are other lexicons that specialize in Greek vocabulary within the Septuagint, in the later Byzantine period, or stretching back into the Classical period (see below). But, for now, being aware of BDAG and seeking to acquire your own personal copy of it is a fitting lexical mission for you.

Are there many abbreviations and notations in BDAG that you will not understand? Yes, a shocking number of them! But the lexicon also has clearly marked,

---

[3] See *A Greek-English Lexicon of the New Testament, Being Grimm's Wilke's Clavis Novi Testamenti*, trans., rev., and enl. Joseph Henry Thayer (New York: American Book, 1889), https://archive.org/details/greekenglishlexi00grimuoft.

numbered definitions (in the 3rd edition!) for every word in the GNT. (If a word only has one main definition, it is in bold text, but it is not numbered.) Bold definitions mark off the "semantic range" or "range of meaning" for each Greek word. Also, you will find Scripture references under the numbered entries, giving the lexicon compilers' judgments about what usages in the GNT reflect the particular meanings listed. (Sometimes you will find the same verse listed under two numbered definitions. Precise lexical decisions can sometimes be difficult!) Focus on what you do understand in the lexicon entry, and don't worry about the rest. For some of you, it will be incredibly difficult to ignore all of the terms and abbreviations that you do not understand. (You know who you are.) Perhaps that frustration you feel is a calling to even deeper study of Greek in the future.

Below, we include a digital entry for a Greek word in BDAG. Skim through the entry and note the four numbered, bold definitions that mark off the range of meaning of the word. Note that there are three subcategories (a., b., c.) under definition #2. Take time to meander through the entry. What other things do you notice in the entry? If you feel comfortable using highlighters in this book, you can mark different features you notice with different colors.

Entry for πειράζω in digital BDAG:

• πειράζω impf. ἐπείραζον; fut. πειράσω; 1 aor. ἐπείρασα, mid. 2 sg. ἐπειράσω. Pass.: 1 aor. ἐπειράσθην; pf. ptc. πεπειρασνένος (fr. πεῖρα; Hom., then Apollon. Rhod. 1, 495; 3, 10. In prose since Philo Mech. 50, 34; 51, 9; also Polyb.; Plut., Cleom. 808 [7, 3], Mor. 230a; Vett. Val. 17, 6; schol. on Aristoph., Pl. 575; PSI 927, 25 [II a.d.]; LXX; TestJos 16:3 v.l.; ApcSed 8:5 p. 133, 5 Ja.; Joseph.; Just., D. 103, 6; 125, 4.—B-D-F §101 p. 54; Mlt-H. 387 n. 1; 404).

1. to make an effort to do someth., ***try, attempt*** at times in a context indicating futility (ὁ θεὸς τῷ πειράζοντι δοὺς ἐξουσίαν τὴν τοῦ διωκειν ἡμᾶς Orig., C. Cels. 8, 70, 11) w. inf. foll. (Polyb. 2, 6, 9; Dt 4:34.—B-D-F §392, 1a) **Ac 9:26**; **16:7**; **24:6**; Hs 8, 2, 7. Foll. by acc. w. inf. IMg 7:1. Abs. Hs 8, 2, 7.

2. to endeavor to discover the nature or character of someth. by testing, ***try, make trial of, put to the test***

a. gener. τινά *someone* (Epict. 1, 9, 29; Ps 25:2) ἑαυτοὺς πειράζετε εἰ ἐστὲ ἐν τῇ πίστει **2 Cor 13:5** (π. εἰ as Jos., Bell. 4, 340). ἐπείρασας τοὺς λέγοντας ἑαυτοὺς ἀποστόλους **Rv 2:2.** προφήτην οὐ πειράσετε οὐδὲ διακρινεῖτε D 11:7.

b. of God or Christ, who put people to the test, in a favorable sense (Ps.-Apollod. 3, 7; 7, 4 Zeus puts τὴν ἀσέβειαν of certain people to the test), so that they may prove themselves true **J 6:6**; **Hb 11:17** (Abraham, as Gen 22:1). Also of painful trials sent by God (Ex 20:20; Dt 8:2 v.l.; Judg 2:22; Wsd 3:5; 11:9; Jdth 8:25f) **1 Cor 10:13**; **Hb 2:18ab**; **4:15** (s. πειράω); **11:37** v.l.; **Rv 3:10** (SBrown, JBL 85, '66, 308–14 π.=*afflict*). Likew. of the measures taken by the angel of repentance Hs 7:1.

c. The Bible (but s. the Pythia in Hdt. 6, 86, 3 τὸ πειρηθῆναι τοῦ θεοῦ κ. τὸ ποιῆσαι ἴσον δύνασθαι 'to have tempted the deity was as bad as doing the deed'; cp. 1, 159) also speaks of a trial of God by humans. Their intent is to put God to the test, to discover whether God really can do a certain thing, esp. whether God notices sin and is able to punish it (Ex 17:2, 7; Num 14:22; Is 7:12; Ps 77:41, 56; Wsd 1:2 al.) **1 Cor 10:9**; **Hb 3:9** (Ps 94:9). τὸ πνεῦμα κυρίου **Ac 5:9.** In **Ac 15:10** the πειράζειν τὸν θεόν consists in the fact that after God's will has been clearly made known through granting of the Spirit to the Gentiles (vs. 8), some doubt and make trial to see whether God's will really becomes operative. τὸν διά σου θεὸν πειράσαι θέλων, εἰ *since I want to put the god (you proclaim) to a test, whether* AcPt Ox 849, 20–22 followed by οὐ πειράζεται ὁ θεός *God refuses to be put to a test.*—ASommer, D. Begriff d. Versuchung im AT u. Judentum, diss. Breslau '35. S. πειράω.

3. to attempt to entrap through a process of inquiry, *test.* Jesus was so treated by his opponents, who planned to use their findings against him **Mt 16:1**; **19:3**; **22:18, 35**; **Mk 8:11**; **10:2**; **12:15**; **Lk 11:16**; **20:23** v.l.; **J 8:6.**

4. to entice to improper behavior, *tempt* Gal 6:1; **Js 1:13a** (s. ἀπό 5eβ) and **b, 14** (Aeschin. 1, 190 the gods do not lead people to sin). Above all the devil works in this way; hence he is directly called ὁ πειράζων *the tempter* **Mt 4:3**; **1 Th 3:5b.** He tempts humans **Ac 5:3** v.l.; **1 Cor 7:5**; **1 Th 3:5a**; **Rv 2:10.** But he also makes bold to tempt Jesus (Just., D. 103, 6; Orig., C. Cels. 6, 43, 28) **Mt 4:1**; **Mk 1:13**; **Lk 4:2** (cp. use of the pass. without ref. to the devil: ἐν τῷ πειράζεσθαι … καὶ σταυροῦσθαι Iren. 3, 19, 3 [Harv. II 104, 3].—Did., Gen. 225, 2). On the temptation of Jesus (s. also **Hb 2:18a**; **4:15**; **2b** above) s. HWillrich, ZNW 4, 1903, 349f; KBornhäuser, Die Versuchungen Jesu nach d. Hb: MKähler Festschr. 1905, 69–86; on this Windisch, Hb[2] '31, 38 exc. on **Hb 4:15**; AHarnack, Sprüche u. Reden Jesu 1907, 32–37; FSpitta, Zur Gesch. u. Lit. des Urchristentums III 2, 1907, 1–108; AMeyer, Die evangel. Berichte üb. d. Vers. Christi: HBlümner Festschr. 1914, 434–68; DVölter, NThT 6, 1917, 348–65; EBöklen, ZNW 18, 1918, 244–48; PKetter, D. Versuchg. Jesu 1918; BViolet, D. Aufbau d. Versuchungsgeschichte Jesu: Harnack Festschr. 1921, 14–21; NFreese, D. Versuchg. Jesu nach den Synopt., diss. Halle 1922, D. Versuchlichkeit Jesu: StKr 96/97, 1925, 313–18; SEitrem/AFridrichsen, D. Versuchg. Christi 1924; Clemen^2 1924, 214–18; HVogels, D. Versuchungen Jesu: BZ 17, 1926, 238–55; SelmaHirsch [s. on βαπτίζω 2a]; HThielicke, Jes. Chr. am Scheideweg '38; PSeidelin, DTh 6, '39, 127–39; HHoughton, On the Temptations of Christ and Zarathustra: ATR 26, '44, 166–75; EFascher, Jesus u. d. Satan '49; RSchnackenburg, TQ 132, '52, 297–326; K-PKöppen, Die Auslegung der Versuchungsgeschichte usw.'61; EBest, The Temptation and the Passion (Mk), '65; JDupont, RB 73, '66, 30–76.—B. 652f. DELG s.v. πεῖρα. M-M. EDNT. DLNT 1166–70. TW. Spicq. Sv.

At this point, you are hopefully thinking, *Wow, I really can use this #1 recommended scholarly resource to give me an understanding of a Greek word's range of meaning. I no longer have to read transliterated Greek and use [fill in the name of inferior resource*]. You may also wonder, *Where can I access this free online?* You cannot. You either need to purchase a print copy (expensive) or purchase the lexicon as a digital module (expensive) within a Bible software program like Logos (see https://www.logos.com). The benefit of having the lexicon in digital format is that, with the click of a computer mouse, you can jump directly from a word in the GNT to its entry in BDAG. Personally, we have both print and digital copies, but then again, we are Bible nerds who write books about doing Greek word studies.

4.4.2 The Theological Dictionary Set We Recommend

We now come to the second of two main resources we are recommending. We could have called it a "theological lexicon set," but as the work's title uses the label "dictionary," we will use that word. How is a theological dictionary/lexicon different from simply a dictionary/lexicon? The theological lexicon goes beyond simply providing a word's semantic range (range of meaning) at a particular time period. A theological lexicon also discusses how a word is employed in significant theological statements in the Christian canon. Remember that to really understand an author's specific meaning intended for a word, the word must be read as part of a statement. Words do not convey specific meaning in isolation from a literary context. In a theological lexicon, it is not uncommon for comparisons and contrasts to be made within the canon. For example, a resource might note that δικαιοσύνη (righteousness) is often employed with a forensic sense (i.e., legally declared righteous) in Paul's writings, but δικαιοσύνη has more of a practical nuance (lived righteousness) in the Gospel of Matthew. Sometimes theological lexicons explore the usage of words in broader Greek literature or in Jewish Greek literature (like the LXX). As they aim to foster theological reflection and synthesis, theological lexicons inevitably reveal the presuppositions of their composers/editors. One of the most influential theological lexicons published in the 1960s–70s in the United States (*Theological Dictionary of the New Testament*, 10 vols., usually referred to as *TDNT* or "Kittel" [the name of the main editor]) evinces an anti-supernaturalism and skepticism toward biblical history. We are not recommending that you use that set! We are recommending a theological dictionary set (5 vols.) edited by a gifted, world-renowned New Testament scholar who is committed to the complete truthfulness of Scripture. And . . . (drumroll), here it is:

> Silva, Moisés, ed. *New International Dictionary of New Testament Theology and Exegesis*. 5 vols. Grand Rapids: Zondervan, 2014.

Silva's *extensive* revision of *The New International Dictionary of New Testament Theology* (ed. Colin Brown, 1975–78) has made a valuable linguistic resource even better. For a pastor or serious Bible student looking for a scholarly, reliable Greek resource with an eye to theological application in the church, *NIDNTTE* is unsurpassed. (And, yes, the set of books is usually referred to as *NIDNTTE*—saying each letter individually, though we have heard someone refer to the set as "Silva." Moisés Silva wrote many other significant works, so it seems potentially confusing to refer to the set with just his name. Also, as Silva himself notes in the introduction to *NIDNTTE*, he is building on the work of many other scholars whose names are listed at the front of the work).

NIDNTTE covers most significant theological words in the GNT, but if you try to look up a word and can't find it, go to volume 5. At the end of volume 5 is the Greek Word Index. Here, you are almost certain to find the word you are looking for, and you will then likely be referred to an entry for a cognate form (form related by the same root) in volume 1–4 of *NIDNTTE*.

NIDNTTE is available in print format or in digital format within some Bible software programs/apps (such as Logos or Olive Tree Bible Study App). The volumes begin with a series of shaded pages that group vocabulary by semantic domain/meaning field, though the very helpful lists are not as extensive as Louw & Nida (see below). The formatting of the digital and print editions of *NIDNTTE* are very similar. We encourage you to have your church purchase a copy of *NIDNTTE* or purchase a copy yourself. Then read all of the *NIDNTTE* entry for πειράζω (the same word we looked at in BDAG). If you are looking in a print edition, you will find the *NIDNTTE* entry for πειράζω on pages 694–703 of volume 3.

There will be things you don't understand. If you want to quickly google an unknown name or word that confuses you, do so. But, on this initial foray into *NIDNTTE*, we suggest that you just skim over parts you don't understand. Even if you only understand half of the entry, you will come away with immeasurable linguistic and theological riches. Please take note of the following features:

(a) The box at the top of the entry lists cognates (words built on the same root) found in the NT. The numbers that are prefixed with a "G" (for example, G4279) are the numbers keyed to the Greek words in the *Zondervan NIV Exhaustive Concordance*, by W. Goodrick and John R. Kohlenberger III. A numbering system like this (also used in Strong's Concordance) enables someone who does not read Greek letters to find all usages of a Greek word in the NT. You, however, do not need to use an English Concordance with a numbering system like this because you can read Greek words! (And the more you practice reading and using Greek words, the easier it will become.) By the way, at this point, you may be wanting to type Greek yourself and have it for your Bible teaching notes. The free website https://www.typegreek.com has a user-friendly interface to help you type Greek in a Unicode font. (Many Greek fonts will appear garbled to you or the person you are sending them to if their computer does not have that Greek font installed, but a Unicode font will not experience that garbling.)

(b) Underneath the box at the top, you will see: "*Concept*: Test." Here Silva is informing you that πειράζω fits in the broader semantic field (meaning category) of "Test." If you flip back to the pages with shading along the edge at the front of the volume, you will find the very helpful "List of Concepts" in alphabetical English order. Since many of you do not own *NIDNTTE* yet, let me tell you what you will find. "Test" is listed like this:

Test, Tempt, Approve (cf. Evil; Lie; Offense; Satan; Sin)

Here, Silva is informing you of related concept words that you could explore in the list. Each one of these concept words will have a listing of Greek words from the NT that fit under the respective category. As we continue reading through the entry for "Test" in the "List of Concepts," we find these Greek words and information listed underneath:

δελεάζω G1284 (*deleazō*), to lure, entice (Jas 1:14; 2 Pet 2:14, 18)
δοκιμάζω G1507 (*dokimazō*), to test, accept as proved, approve
†πειράζω G4279 (*peirazō*), to try, test, put on trial, tempt
σκανδαλίζω G4997 (*skandalizō*), to make to stumble, give offense, lead astray, cause to sin, pass. fall into sin (→ σκάνδαλον G4998)

Silva explains the dagger symbol (†) before a word: "A dagger (†, used at least once for most concepts, but not for all of them) indicates the articles that contain the main discussions of a particular concept, usually accompanied by a fuller bibliography."

(c) As you quickly skim over the rest of the entry for πειράζω, you will notice it is divided into three large sections marked by bold, indented capital letters on the left: **GL**, **JL**, and **NT**. **GL** stands for General (Greek) Literature. Here, Silva explores the meaning of πειράζω in non-biblical Greek literature. Attention is given to the history of the word in earlier time periods, but not in the simplistic way of the "etymological fallacy." Silva is a master linguist, and if you read the introduction to *NIDNTTE* in volume 1 of the set, you will see that he is very deliberate and nuanced in his approach. **JL** stands for Jewish literature and looks at the use of πειράζω in Greek Jewish literature from mainly the Koine period. Here, you will encounter the names of some documents and authors with which you are unfamiliar. When you are holding a print volume in your hand, it's advisable to keep one finger on the abbreviations key at the front of the book. Silva sometimes discusses the underlying Hebrew or Aramaic words from which the Greek word under investigation is translated. We expect only a handful of you to be able to read Hebrew, but as long as you don't let the actual Hebrew words intimidate you, you will actually be able to follow much of the discussion. Remember that in academic writing of this sort, some views and examples are given for comparison. Not every ancient usage or scholar quoted is intended to be followed or applied to the NT. Scholarly writing is prone to understatement and nuance. You need to read the entire dictionary entry before you can be confident why Silva is discussing a particular ancient example or modern scholar's thoughts. **NT** stands for New Testament, the section in which Silva focuses on the use of πειράζω in the NT. Notice how he is concerned with reflecting the diversity of usage in the canon. (Wow! Think how much you are learning. Isn't learning to do real Greek word studies amazing?)

(d) Note the bibliography at the end of the entry. Many of the sources are technical academic journals or in foreign languages. Obviously, most of the readers of this book will not find the *NIDNTTE* bibliographies helpful.

(e) Finally, an abbreviated version of Silva's five-volume work is now available. It is called *The Concise New International Dictionary of New Testament Theology and Exegesis* (2021), edited by Christopher A. Beetham. This one-volume version consists of 1,200 pages and retains the essentials of Silva's work.

4.4.3 A Lexicon Based on Semantic Domains

Although it is not one of our top two recommendations, we want to commend to you the value of another lexical resource. Do you remember in chapter 2 when we spoke about the danger of confusing a word with its concept? There, we spoke about performing a search on a single word such as προσεύχομαι (pray, *verb*) and erroneously concluding that one has done an exhaustive study of prayer in the GNT. In fact, many Greek words refer to prayer in the GNT. Is there some resource that you would expect to list all the Greek words on prayer side by side and show the different nuances between them? Well, *NIDNTTE* does that in abbreviated form with the "List of Concepts" at the front of each volume. A resource that fills out in more detail a mapping of those semantic domains (meaning fields) is:

> Louw, Johannes P., and Eugene A. Nida. *Greek-English Lexicon of the New Testament Based on Semantic Domains*, 2 vols. New York: United Bible Societies, 1988.

Unfortunately, in recent years, these two volumes have been out of print, but they are still widely available in digital format within Bible software programs (see https://www.logos.com). You've likely noticed that biblical scholars often refer to their tools with abbreviations, and this work is no exception. It is usually called "Louw & Nida." Both volumes are essential (if you are using a print edition), because the second volume lists Greek words in alphabetical order. So, for example, if you look up the word προσεύχομαι (pray, *verb*) in volume 2, the resource will provide you with a number for a "meaning category" in which similar words will be grouped in volume 1. Volume 1 is not organized alphabetically, but according to "semantic domain" (meaning category/field). So, if you don't start with volume 2, you won't know where to look for your word in volume 1. When I (Rob) looked up προσεύχομαι in volume 2, it directed me to volume 1, the domain for "Communication" (Domain 33), in Subdomain 178–179 (Pray). When I looked up §§33.178–179 in volume 1 of Louw & Nida, I was initially disappointed by the sparse listing of Greek forms. There was however a helpful footnote which read:

> In addition to the expressions listed in this subdomain, there are others which are often translated "to pray" or "prayer," namely, ἐρωτάω (33.161), αἰτέω (33.163), δέομαι (33.170) and δέησις (33.171), used exclusively of urgent requests to God and thus normally translated "prayer," though these terms do not mean "prayer" in and of themselves. The gloss "prayer" translates their contextual usage.

Louw & Nida was created to assist Bible translators, which helps clarify why some of the definitions are worded oddly. (For example, a definition frequently may say something like, "In some languages, a plural form of this word may not exist, so the translator can . . ."). A free partial digital version of Louw & Nida can be accessed here: https://www.laparola.net/greco/louwnida.php.

4.5 DECENT GREEK WORD STUDY TOOLS THAT ARE FREE

Although you can freely access a partial version of Louw & Nida online, you must pay to purchase a digital or print copy. (And, sadly, as of the writing of this chapter, only over-priced used print copies are available online.) BDAG and *NIDNTTE* are also not cheap. Are there any free resources we can recommend? The items we recommend above are the best, so you should seek to use those, but we realize that some readers might not be able to purchase them right away. So, recognizing that challenge, we recommend the following:

Thayer, Joseph Henry. *A Greek-English Lexicon of the New Testament, Being Grimm's Wilke's Clavis Novi Testamenti*. Translated, revised, and enlarged by Joseph Henry Thayer, D.D. (Edinburgh: T&T Clark, 1896).[4]

Referred to as simply "Thayer's," this lexicon was a standard resource for many decades in seminaries. It has been surpassed by the precision and comprehensiveness of BDAG. Thayer's is in the public domain, so the definitions from the lexicon are often found hyperlinked to Greek words in free online versions of the GNT. If you want to virtually flip through a scanned version of the print edition of Thayer's, you can do so on the Internet Archive (See: https://archive.org/details/greekenglishlexi00grimuoft).

Bill Mounce's Free Online Greek Dictionary

Senior Greek scholar Bill Mounce is seeking to create a reliable, free, online Greek dictionary that can be used for definitions in online GNTs. Currently, there is still a lot of work to be done in filling out the definitions, but it's an admirable goal. See: https://www.billmounce.com/greek-dictionary.

4.6 GREEK WORD STUDY TOOLS FOR MORE ADVANCED STUDENTS

Most of you will never need to acquire or reference the volumes listed below. A few of you will salivate at the possibilities and perhaps will eventually purchase some of the following resources. Most of these items are available in both print and digital format.

- **Balz, H., and G. Schneider. *Exegetical Dictionary of the New Testament*, 3 vols. Grand Rapids: Eerdmans, 1990–93**. *EDNT*, a translation and revision of a German lexicon, is an excellent dictionary set that covers the entire vocabulary of the GNT but focuses attention on significant theological terms.
- **Beekes, Robert. *Etymological Dictionary of Greek*. Leiden Indo-European Etymological Dictionary Series 10. Leiden: Brill, 2010**. This

[4] The title is so strange because it's an older volume, and Thayer and his publishers wanted to give rightful credit to the previous work of others that he translated, revised, and enlarged.

two-volume dictionary set is the most authoritative source for the etymology of Greek words. This work is aimed at Classical Greek, though many of the words occur in the NT as well. Much of the discussion is technical.

- **Kittel, G., and G. Friedrich, eds. *Theological Dictionary of the New Testament*, 10 vols. Translated and edited by G. W. Bromiley. Grand Rapids: Eerdmans, 1964–76**. *TDNT* or "Kittel" is not an exhaustive dictionary but concentrates on terms with theological significance. This work gives extensive treatment of the usage of the term in the LXX, and early Judaism. *TDNT* groups cognate terms together. Many articles in *TDNT* were written by Germans with liberal theological predilections and therefore must be read with caution.
- **Liddell, Henry George, and Robert Scott. *A Greek-English Lexicon with a Revised Supplement*. Revised and augmented by Henry Stuart Jones. Oxford: Clarendon, 1996**. This is an indispensable lexicon for working in Greek literature outside the NT, especially from the classical period. This lexicon is referred to with a variety of abbreviations and identifiers—LSJ, Liddell-Scott-Jones, or simply Liddell-Scott. There is a shortened version of LSJ sometimes called "Middle Liddell" and an even further abbreviated version called "Little Liddell." The full-length LSJ was intended as a comprehensive lexicon of ancient Greek and does give LXX and NT word meanings in many of its entries.
- **Lust, J., E. Eynikel, and K. Hauspie, eds. *A Greek-English Lexicon of the Septuagint*. Rev. ed. Stuttgart: Deutsche Bibelgesellschaft, 2003**. This is one of two significant lexicons for the Septuagint or LXX. This work is sometimes called Lust-Eynikel-Hauspie or LEH. In LEH definitions, the editors are asking this question: "Based upon translation technique, what is the meaning intended by the *translators* of the LXX?"
- **Montanari, Franco, ed. *The Brill Dictionary of Ancient Greek*. Edited by Madeleine Goh, Chad Matthew Schroeder, Gregory Nagy, and Leonard Muellner. Translated by Rachel Barritt-Costa. Leiden: Brill, 2015**. Heralded by some scholars as "the new LSJ" (see above) and criticized by others as LSJ recycled (through Italian and back into English), *The Brill Dictionary of Ancient Greek* is still being assessed by scholars. I (Rob) have personally found the formatting appealing and information useful in the few times I have used it. The work is intended to cover both

the Classical and Koine periods. Perhaps the dominant way to refer to this new lexicon is "BrillDAG" (pronounced as two syllables—Brill-Dag).

- **Moulton, J. H., and G. Milligan.** ***The Vocabulary of the Greek New Testament.*** **Peabody, MA: Hendrickson, 1997**. This dictionary, originally published as one volume in 1930 by Hodder & Stoughton (London), gives information on NT words based on ancient papyri and inscriptions. A Scripture index can be found in the back. This work is referred to as "Moulton & Milligan," and since the original work is in the public domain, a scan of it may be viewed legally on the internet archive.[5] Canadian linguist Allan Loder has spent years revising and expanding Moulton & Milligan. The ongoing revision, known as *Vocabulary of the Greek New Testament: Student Edition* (*VGNTS*), is currently available for download only on the Word Bible Software homepage (https://theword.net/). *VGNTS* should be more widely available in print and digital formats soon.
- **Muraoka, T.** ***A Greek-English Lexicon of the Septuagint.*** **Leuven: Peeters, 2009**. This is the other major lexicon for the Septuagint. Muraoka looks to secular Greek sources as the background for the meaning of words in the LXX. In his definitions, Muraoka is asking, "How did an *early reader* (who had no access to the parent text of the LXX) understand these words?"
- ***New Documents Illustrating Early Christianity.*** **Sydney, Australia: Macquarie University, 1981–present**. As of 2023 the Ancient History Documentary Research Centre of Macquarie University, Sydney, Australia, has published 10 volumes of *NewDocs*. This series continues the Moulton & Milligan tradition of illustrating the meaning of NT Greek words through ancient papyri and inscriptions. The first volume of *NewDocs* (published in 1981 by Liverpool University Press) discusses inscriptions and papyri published in 1976. The most recent volume of *NewDocs* was published in 2012 by Eerdmans and discusses papyri and inscriptions published between 1988–1992.
- **Spicq, Ceslas.** ***Theological Lexicon of the New Testament.*** **Translated and edited by James D. Ernest. Peabody, MA: Hendrickson, 1994**.

[5] https://archive.org/details/vocabularyofgree00mouluoft.

Translated from French, this 3-volume lexicon was prepared by the famous linguist Ceslas Spicq. The work provides a series of short studies on theologically significant words in the GNT.

- ***Thesaurus Linguae Graecae***. (stephanus.tlg.uci.edu) Known as *TLG* and overseen by the University of California, Irvine, this database currently boasts a comprehensive, searchable collection of Greek writings from the time of Homer to the fall of Byzantium in AD 1453. As access to *TLG* requires an online subscription, most students access it via a seminary or college library account.

4.7 CAVEAT: DO NOT VIEW WORD STUDY TOOLS AS INERRANT

The number of excellent Greek word study tools available is intoxicating. At the same time, we must remember that these resources were created by fallible human beings who sometimes show their mental frailty or theological biases. Louw and Nida's *Greek-English Lexicon of the New Testament Based on Semantic Domains* is an excellent resource, but like all such resources, it is not perfect. For example, under the word λόγος, Louw and Nida rightly list "gospel" as one of the potential meanings of the word.[6] Under the word ῥῆμα, however, "gospel" is not listed as a possible meaning,[7] even though ῥῆμα carries those connotations in multiple contexts (e.g., Rom 10:8, 17, 18; Eph 5:26; 6:17).

Theological bias can also show up in lexicons. In the entry for ἱλασμός, Louw and Nida argue against the English rendering "propitiation" (wrath-appeasing) because "in the NT God is never the object of propitiation since he is already on the side of people."[8] While the idea that God is not wrathful toward sinners may be popular in certain theological circles, it directly contradicts NT teaching and is not based on linguistic evidence.[9]

To remind myself of the fallible nature of Greek lexicons, I (Rob) keep a hand-written list of my suggested corrections on the blank pages in the back of

---

[6] Louw & Nida, 2:153.

[7] Louw & Nida, 2:217.

[8] Louw & Nida, 1:504 (§40.12).

[9] E.g., John 3:36, "The one who believes in the Son has eternal life, but the one who rejects the Son will not see life; instead, the wrath of God remains on him" (see also Rom 1:18).

my lexicons. If you use digital lexicons, perhaps you could keep a digital file of your critiques.

4.8 VOCABULARY

βλέπω	I see, look at
διδάσκω	I teach (didactic)
ἐγείρω	I raise up
κρίνω	I judge, condemn (critic)
δοῦλος	slave (doula)
θάνατος	death ("Thanatopsis," poem by William Cullen Bryant)
ὥρα	hour (hour)

4.9 PRACTICE EXERCISES[10]

A. Writing: Practice handwriting and pronouncing your new Greek vocabulary words. Review your old words too. Write out the Greek alphabet from memory.

βλέπω ____________________
διδάσκω ____________________
ἐγείρω ____________________
κρίνω ____________________
δοῦλος ____________________
θάνατος ____________________
ὥρα ____________________

B. Lexicon: Look up the following words in BDAG and record the numbered definitions for each. (Remember, if only one bold definition is given, it is not numbered). If you cannot access BDAG, then use the free, online

[10] Videos featuring a textbook author working through the practice exercises are found at https://www.wordstudiesforeveryone.com. Before accessing those videos, you should (1) study the material in this chapter and (2) attempt the activities without reference to the videos.

scan of Thayer's lexicon on the internet archive: https://archive.org/details/greekenglishlexi00grimuoft. It will be good for you to practice flipping through a lexicon, even if that flipping is just done virtually via a digital scan on the internet archive.

- ἀσέλγεια
- ἐκπίπτω
- καταργέω
- ποιμήν
- τρέχω

C. **Theological Dictionary**: Look up the following words in *NIDNTTE*. Read all of each entry and write a brief list of helpful insights. Alternately, if you cannot access *NIDNTTE*, then use the free, online scan of Thayer's lexicon on the internet archive: https://archive.org/details/greekenglishlexi00grimuoft.

- κλέπτω
- οἶκος
- σοφία

CHAPTER 5

/////////////////

THE IMPORTANCE OF A CONCORDANCE

We recommend watching the video lecture before reading the chapter. The QR code and link to the video can be found on page x.

5.1 OVERVIEW

Perhaps you've heard people speak of the legendary "Strong's Concordance" for years. But what is a concordance and why would someone use one? How does a concordance help with Bible study, or more specifically, how does a concordance help with word studies in the Bible? We will be answering these questions in this chapter. We will also survey a bit more of the Greek grammatical system, while also addressing this question: why are we not trying to teach you more Greek grammar now?

5.2 SIGNIFICANCE

In 1 John 2:15, John commands, μὴ **ἀγαπᾶτε** τὸν **κόσμον** ("Do not **love** the **world**"). In John 3:16, the apostle famously writes, οὕτως γὰρ **ἠγάπησεν** ὁ θεὸς τὸν **κόσμον** ("For God so **loved** the **world**" ESV). Students of Greek will note that, in both passages, the verbs translated "love" (ἀγαπάω) and the nouns translated "world" (κόσμος) are derived from the same respective lexical forms.

Are Christians, then, commanded *not* to do something ("love the world") that God does?

First John 2:15 and John 3:16 illustrate that every word has a range of meaning (a semantic range) and also a specific meaning that can only be determined when considering the context in which the word is used. In 1 John 2:15–16, the apostle's explanatory comments clarify how we should understand his command not to love the world. John writes,

> ἐάν τις ἀγαπᾷ τὸν κόσμον, οὐκ ἔστιν ἡ ἀγάπη τοῦ πατρὸς ἐν αὐτῷ· ὅτι πᾶν τὸ ἐν τῷ κόσμῳ, ἡ ἐπιθυμία τῆς σαρκὸς καὶ ἡ ἐπιθυμία τῶν ὀφθαλμῶν καὶ ἡ ἀλαζονεία τοῦ βίου, οὐκ ἔστιν ἐκ τοῦ πατρὸς ἀλλ' ἐκ τοῦ κόσμου ἐστίν.

> If anyone loves the world, the love of the Father is not in him. For everything in the world—the lust of the flesh, the lust of the eyes, and the pride in one's possessions—is not from the Father, but is from the world.

Thus, the "love" that John speaks of in 1 John 2:15 ("Do not love the world") stands in contrast with devotion to God and is characterized by the lust and boastful pride of humanity's fallen nature. Similarly, "the world" here must mean the things in this world that entice and gratify the longings of humanity's sinful nature. "Do not love the world" (1 John 2:15) means "Do not sinfully long to satisfy yourself with the blandishments of this wicked, fallen order."

With significantly different contextual clues in John 3:16b–17, the apostle clarifies both who "the world" is and the way in which (οὕτως) God loved this world. John writes:

> ὥστε τὸν υἱὸν τὸν μονογενῆ ἔδωκεν, ἵνα πᾶς ὁ πιστεύων εἰς αὐτὸν μὴ ἀπόληται ἀλλ' ἔχῃ ζωὴν αἰώνιον. οὐ γὰρ ἀπέστειλεν ὁ θεὸς τὸν υἱὸν εἰς τὸν κόσμον ἵνα κρίνῃ τὸν κόσμον, ἀλλ' ἵνα σωθῇ ὁ κόσμος δι' αὐτοῦ.

> He gave his one and only Son, so that everyone who believes in him will not perish but have eternal life. For God did not send his Son into the world to condemn the world, but to save the world through him.

So, in John 3:16–17, "the world" is not the sinful allurements of this fallen age, but humans in their desperate lost state. God's "loving" these sinful humans speaks of his activity and desire to rescue them. All words have a range of meaning, and the broader literary context is crucial for determining a word's or phrase's meaning in any given passage.

5.3 WHAT IS A CONCORDANCE (AND A CONCORDANCE-TYPE DIGITAL SEARCH)?

A concordance is a book that lists all occurrences of words from a particular body of literature in alphabetical order. For instance, if we flipped open a Bible concordance to the letter "K," we might see all occurrences of "king" listed in the order they appear in the Bible, followed by all instances of "kingdom," followed by "kingly," followed by "kings," and so on. It is typical for a concordance to include a few surrounding words with each citation so a researcher can quickly see the word occurrences in context.

Strong's Concordance lists every single word in the King James Bible. Since it includes every word, it is an "exhaustive" concordance. (It is a very heavy book, so it can also be *exhausting* to carry around!) Some concordances just focus on more significant vocabulary words. There are also concordances based on different modern translations of the English Bible. Concordances can show you how a word reappears and is employed differently (or in the same way) by various biblical authors. Of course, when you are using an English concordance, additional steps are required. Each English word entry also includes a number that identifies the underlying Greek word. Then, the researcher needs to flip to the back of the concordance to find the specific Greek word, as well as discovering what other ways that word has been translated into English. Then, the researcher needs to flip back to the other English words translated by that Greek word and look for the specific examples that match the number for the exact Greek word you are investigating. With quite a bit of flipping, the researcher can come up with a list of all Bible verses that contain a particular Greek word. There are some online tools that can simplify the flipping process of a printed concordance, but wouldn't it be easier (with less potential for error) just to use a Greek concordance directly based on the GNT? Yes! That's why we pushed you to learn to read Greek!

With a printed Greek concordance, there is no additional required flipping. When you look up the Greek word θησαυρίζω ("store up, gather") in a concordance of the GNT, the volume lists all eight occurrences of the word in the GNT.

With each occurrence of θησαυρίζω, we find about 5–10 of the surrounding words from verses referenced so a researcher can quickly see the context.

Printed concordances are in rapid decline. Now, with the click of a mouse, a Bible software program or many free online GNT websites will list all occurrences of a Greek word in the GNT or the LXX. These searches are sometimes listed as "*lemma*" searches, which sounds confusing, but it just means you want to see every instance of the word, regardless of how its spelling has changed in different forms.

5.4 WHY SHOULD I DO A CONCORDANCE-TYPE SEARCH?

A lexicon can give you the range of meaning of a particular Greek word, but it's very valuable to see that Greek word actually employed in different contexts. As you do careful concordance studies, you may conclude that some lexicon definitions should be nuanced slightly to account for the actual evidence you are seeing.

Pieces of literature that are closer in time period and worldview are often the most helpful in elucidating similar word usage. For example, when we want to better understand how the word πειράζω ("test, tempt") is used in Matthew 4:3, we don't use a concordance for *The Histories*, by the ancient Greek historian Herodotus (c. 484–c. 425 BC). Instead, we use a concordance of the GNT. Moreover, we will give priority to Matthew's other instances of the word, although we don't simplistically think that each instance of the same Greek word in his writing must have the same nuances. Then, we look at uses of πειράζω throughout the GNT both to see the word's range of meaning and to find instances that correspond more directly with the context of a passage we are investigating.

After we finish with the GNT, where do we go from there? The most important background literature of the GNT is the early Greek translation of the Old Testament that early Christians used as their Bible. We have mentioned it in this book several times already. It is normally called the Septuagint or the LXX. With Bible software programs or free online GNT websites, it's easy to search a concordance of the LXX for additional instances of the Greek word we are studying. A small warning—the versification of the Septuagint sometimes differs from the English Bible versification slightly. If you need to check the versification of the LXX with your findings (or perhaps read in English the OT Greek verse where the word you are searching for appears), here is a link to a free English translation of the Septuagint: https://ccat.sas.upenn.edu/nets/edition/.

If you have a Bible software program, you can purchase digital copies of other Greek texts from around the time of the GNT, which can often provide further helpful examples of synchronous (same-time) Greek word usage. Following are three texts that can be used this way:

- **The writings of Philo**. Philo (c. 20 BC–AD 50) was a Jewish writer who sought to synthesize Greek philosophical thought and the Jewish Scriptures.
- **The writings of Josephus**. Flavius Josephus (c. AD 37–100) was a Pharisee and fought the Romans. After surrendering to the Romans, he ended up receiving favor from the emperor and wrote a variety of historical and apologetic works.
- **The Apostolic Fathers**. The Apostolic Fathers (c. AD 70–150, by various authors) is the earliest collection of Christian documents written after the GNT.

With the click of a mouse, an ancient author's entire collection of works may be searched in a concordance-type fashion. If you do not know Greek well enough to read the Greek text (and we assume you don't, since you are reading this book), it is easy to display side-by-side an English translation of Philo, Josephus, or the Apostolic Fathers.

5.5 EXAMPLES OF CONCORDANCE-TYPE SEARCHES

Paul wrote Philemon to ask him to welcome back his runaway slave Onesimus no longer as a slave, but as a brother. The rhetorical escalation in the letter is masterful, but it is even more striking in Greek. When you read through Paul's letter to Philemon, you will notice that Paul calls Onesimus "my very own heart" (v. 12). The underlying Greek word here intrigues you, so you check it out. It is the plural form of σπλάγχνον, and a glance at the BDAG lexicon tells you that the word can mean (1) physical entrails or bowels. (Be sure to read the KJV translation of Philemon verse 12 to a group of middle school boys.) Definitions #2 and #3 add further insight to our investigation:

2. as often in the ancient world, inner body parts served as referents for psychological aspects (s. καρδία [heart]): of the seat of the emotions, in our usage a transference is made to the rendering ***heart***
3. of the feeling itself, pl. ***love, affection***

Obviously, Paul is not intending the word σπλάγχνα in a literal way (in contrast to the way we see it used in Acts 1:18). Rather, the apostle is calling Onesimus his dearly loved one. A quick concordance-type search reveals that σπλάγχνα occurs only eleven times in the GNT, and three of those uses are in this short letter of Paul to Philemon (vv. 7, 12, 20)! If you look at the context of the other verses in the GNT that include σπλάγχνα, the word appears to convey a deep sense of emotion. (Would "the deepest part" be an over-translation?) Καρδία is the normal Greek word translated as "heart," and it occurs 156 times in the GNT. Highlight the three instances of σπλάγχνα in Paul's letter to Philemon and read back through the correspondence. Consider how this rare and emotionally charged word functions in Paul's appeal.

Let's consider another word study in which a concordance-type search into a broader body of Greek literature proves helpful. Let's imagine that you are preparing a Bible study lesson on Luke 21. As you study verse 34, you come upon a puzzling word, κραιπάλη. As this word only occurs once in the NT, you have likely never seen it. The CSB translates verses 34–36 as:

> Be on your guard, so that your minds are not dulled from <u>carousing</u>, drunkenness, and worries of life, or that day will come on you unexpectedly like a trap. For it will come on all who live on the face of the whole earth. But be alert at all times, praying that you may have strength to escape all these things that are going to take place and to stand before the Son of Man. (underlining added)

"*Carousing*?" you think. *What is carousing*? In context, Jesus is warning against sinful behaviors that should not mark his followers as they await his return. Clearly, "carousing" is a negative term. (Literary context is foundationally important!) Whatever this word means, it is something that Jesus condemns. Also, we note specifically that Jesus warns against their minds (Greek: ὑμῶν αἱ καρδίαι, lit. "your hearts") being weighed down (βαρηθῶσιν) or dulled by carousing, drunkenness, and worries.

How do other English Bible translations render κραιπάλη? This can be a helpful step in word studies that we have not done yet. Modern English Bible translations are composed with extreme care and thoughtfulness, so we do not want to neglect the insights of the scholarly committees that stand behind our modern translations.

ENGLISH BIBLE VERSION	RENDERING OF κραιπάλη
Common English Bible	"drinking parties"
English Standard Version	"dissipation"
King James Version	"surfeiting"
New International Reader's Version	"wasteful living"
New Jerusalem Bible	"debauchery"
New Living Translation	"carousing"

Interestingly, most Bible translations (except for the CEB and NIRV) render κραιπάλη with an obscure English word. Arguably, most modern readers would not understand the meaning of "surfeiting," "debauchery," or "dissipation." In a modern dictionary, all of these words have, as part of their range of meaning, the nuance of excessive alcohol consumption. Though this alcohol-specific meaning is apparently intended by the translators of the various English translations noted above, in dictionaries of modern English, excessive drinking is sometimes listed as a secondary or archaic definition of the word in question.[1] Although the meaning of the English word "carousing" matches closely the meaning of the underlying Greek term (as we will see), the word "carousing" is poorly understood and rarely used in modern English.

The NIRV's translation ("wasteful living") is understandable but ambiguous. Does "wasteful living" refer to wasting money? Wasting natural resources? Wasting one's potential? The CEB's "drinking parties" is by far the most understandable translation, but is it accurate? Does κραιπάλη refer not just to excessive drinking, but immoderate drinking and wild behavior in a group setting?

In the final version cited in the chart above (the NLT), the punctuation and translation imply that the translators understand "drunkenness" (μέθη, Luke 21:34) as connected tightly with "carousing" (κραιπάλη). The NLT reads, "By carousing and drunkenness, and by the worries of this life." In other words, "carousing and drunkenness" are likely being presented by the NLT translators as a hendiadys, that is, two terms used to express one underlying reality. For example, if someone says, "That man has plunged into wickedness and sin," you do not understand them as referring to two realities—that is, that the man plunged into (1) wickedness and then (possibly at a later time), also plunged into (2) sin. Rather, the phrase

[1] See, for example, *Merriam-Webster.com*, s.v. "dissipation," definition 1d, accessed February 27, 2024, https://www.merriam-webster.com/dictionary/dissipation.

"wickedness and sin" refers to one reality, and the speaker likely employs two near synonyms to intensify or possibly slightly broaden the reference.

At this point, you will likely want to consider the definition(s) of κραιπάλη found in the two main word study tools we recommended to you.

- **BDAG**: "both 'carousing, intoxication' and its result 'drunken headache, hangover' are associated in the use of the term, since it means 'dizziness, staggering' when the head refuses to function . . . **unbridled indulgence in a drinking party**, ***drinking bout*** . . ." [bold and italics original].[2]
- ***NIDNTTE*** has an insightful discussion of various Greek words for drunkenness and the broader NT teaching on inebriation in volume 3, pages 258–60. In considering the Greek terms for drunkenness, *NIDNTTE* discusses briefly the historical and cultural context, as well as metaphorical uses of the words. Silva provides some theological synthesis on the NT's teaching on drunkenness, as well as noting linguistic patterns (e.g., "the noun μέθη ['drunkenness'] occurs 3x alongside synonyms").[3]

When you attempt a concordance-type search of κραιπάλη, you find there are no other occurrences of the word in the NT or LXX. Because you invested in a good Bible software program, additional searches in synchronous (from the same time period) Greek literature are relatively easy. A search of the Apostolic Fathers turns up one occurrence in Hermas *Mandate* 6.2.5.[4] There an angelic messenger instructs an early Christian named Hermas:

> ὅταν ὀξυχολία σοί τις προσπέσῃ ἢ πικρία γίνωσκε ὅτι αὐτός ἐστιν ἐν σοί εἶτα ἐπιθυμία πράξεων πολλῶν καὶ πολυτέλειαι ἐδεσμάτων πολλῶν καὶ μεθυσμάτων καὶ **κραιπαλῶν** πολλῶν καὶ ποικίλων τρυφῶν καὶ οὐ δεόντων καὶ ἐπιθυμίαι γυναικῶν καὶ πλεονεξία καὶ ὑπερηφανία πολλή τις καὶ ἀλαζονεία καὶ ὅσα τούτοις παραπλήσιά ἐστι καὶ ὅμοια ταῦτα οὖν ὅταν ἐπὶ τὴν καρδίαν σου ἀναβῇ γίνωσκε ὅτι ὁ ἄγγελος τῆς πονηρίας ἐστὶν ἐν σοι (bold added)

Michael Holmes translates the above passage as follows:

---

[2] BDAG, 564.

[3] *NIDNTTE*, 3:259.

[4] Also cited in BDAG's entry for κραιπάλη (564).

> When some angry temperamental outburst or bitterness comes over you, recognize that [the angel of wickedness] is in you. Then comes the desire for much business, and extravagant kinds of foods and drink, and much drunkenness, and various kinds of unnecessary luxuries, and the desire for women, and greed and arrogance and pretentiousness, and whatever else resembles or is similar to these things. So whenever these things enter your heart, you know that the angel of wickedness is with you.[5]

From this passage, it is clear that κραιπάλη is a word that belongs in Christian "vice lists," along with greed and arrogance. We are right to see it as a behavior evaluated negatively by early Christians. It is interesting that, unlike the occurrence in Luke 21:34, here κραιπάλη occurs in the plural with the modifier πολύς ("much"). Because the context provides little detail, it is difficult to say much more about the word.

No occurrence of κραιπάλη turns up in Josephus, but the word is found once in Philo's "On the Posterity and Exile of Cain."[6] In this text, Philo discusses the drunken behavior of Lot whereby he impregnated his two daughters (Gen 19:30–38). The word κραιπάλη is connected with immoral behavior accompanying the stupor of extreme drunkenness.

Looking at the various instances of κραιπάλη, you conclude that the word refers not just to drunkenness in the abstract, but visible immoral behavior that often accompanies the clouded faculties of an inebriated person. The ancient texts above present such immoral behavior in relation to other persons, that is, the way a drunk person sins against others through foolish talk, violence, and sexual exploitation.

In Luke 21:34–36, Jesus warns about the things that can dull the hearts and minds of his followers as they await his return. One of these is anxiety or worry. And indeed, forgetting there is a sovereign Lord who will return to right all wrongs could lead one to frightful anxiety. Another false spiritual path is escapism—drinking and partying, "living it up." Neither despair nor escapism is the Christian response to the current broken world, but faithful and prayerful discipleship. In preparing a Bible

---

[5] Michael W. Holmes, ed., *The Apostolic Fathers: Greek Texts and English Translations* (Grand Rapids: Baker, 2007), 523–24 (bold font added).

[6] *De posteritate Caini*, 1.176. For an affordable English translation of this text, see *The Works of Philo: New Updated Edition*, trans. C. D. Yonge (Peabody, MA: Hendrickson, 1993), 150.

lesson on Luke 21:34–36, one will want to consider other forms of escapism that are treated in the Bible, especially those that capture the hearts of people to whom you are ministering. For example, many people find meaning through parading their wealth and success (1 John 2:16). Not only drunkenness, but the idolatry of prestige and luxury can intoxicate us and render us ineffective and unfaithful.

5.6 DIGITAL CONCORDANCES OF THE GNT AND LXX

Within a Bible software program (for example, Logos), you can easily search for the lemma of a word (i.e., a concordance-type search). Numerous free online GNT programs will also do concordance-type searches. We will list a few such programs below. In the free video lectures that accompany this textbook, we demonstrate how to do some of these concordance-type searches with the free programs. Sometimes websites shut down, but we will seek to keep the online video training for this textbook up-to-date, even if the websites listed below close down.

- **https://lexicon.katabiblon.com**. You need to come to this website knowing the lexical form of the Greek word that you want to search for in the GNT and LXX. Then, using the digital buttons, navigate your way to the word. When you click on the word, it will open up a link to the Liddell-Scott-Jones lexicon entry, as well as a list of all occurrences of the word in the GNT and LXX. Be sure to scroll down the entire webpage to see all the helpful information.
- **https://app.biblearc.com**. When you click on a Greek word in the GNT or LXX, a box with additional information will open up. Click on the magnifying glass (search) symbol in the upper right of that box. It will give you the option to search for all forms of the word in either the GNT or LXX. If you are searching on the GNT text only, additional options may be given to you—for example to only search in Paul's letters.
- **The Greek New Testament Study App**. Download this free app to your mobile device. Once you have the program on your phone or tablet, simply click on a word in the GNT, and a blue box will open up. If you click on the number in the upper righthand corner of that box, it will take you to a total number of all occurrences of that word in the GNT. Click on "X occurrences" to have the verses listed for viewing.

5.7 PRINTED CONCORDANCES OF THE GNT AND LXX

Are there printed concordances of the GNT and the LXX? Yes! But with the advent of quick, free concordance-type searches of the same data online, hardly anyone uses a printed concordance anymore. Publishers are not inclined to keep books in print that few people buy. And, sadly, such books are usually quite expensive. Following are two printed concordances of the GNT of which we are aware:

- John R. Kohlenberger III, Edward W. Goodrick, and James A. Swanson, eds. *The Exhaustive Concordance to the Greek New Testament*. Grand Rapids: Zondervan, 1995.
- W. F. Moulton and A.S. Geden, eds. *A Concordance to the Greek New Testament*. 6th ed., edited by I. Howard Marshall (1897; London: T&T Clark, 2004).

The classic printed concordance of the LXX is:

- Edwin Hatch and Henry A. Redpath, eds. *A Concordance to the Septuagint and Other Greek Versions of the Old Testament (Including the Apocryphal Books)*. 2nd ed. (Oxford: Clarendon, 1906; repr., Grand Rapids: Baker, 1991).

Known as "Hatch & Redpath," this work is in the public domain. A digital scan of the print volume is available on the internet archive:

https://archive.org/details/aconcordancetos00redpgoog

Works in the public domain are rarely profitable for a publisher to print, but every decade or so, a publisher reprints Hatch & Redpath.

There is something delightful about the experience of turning physical pages and seeing words on a surface that is not glowing back at you. Considering that reality, a few of you may wish to acquire print concordances of the GNT and LXX. Nevertheless, most of you will be content to use free, quicker (and perhaps more accurate) digital searches to find all occurrences of a Greek word in the GNT or LXX. We should note that while the databases that underlie the Greek online resources above are very accurate, there can be occasional errors. Every database is ultimately based on data entered by humans, and sometimes humans make mistakes!

5.8 EXCURSUS: WHY ARE WE NOT TRYING TO TEACH YOU MORE GREEK GRAMMAR NOW?

Some of you are eager to learn more specifics of Greek grammar, but that is not the purpose of this book. This volume is intended to bring you to an entry-level competency in using the best Greek word study resources. Below, we are going to include a very brief overview of Greek nouns and verbs. The overview will demonstrate that Greek nouns and verbs will change in spelling a great deal. So, don't be surprised if you search for all occurrences of a word in the GNT, and the forms that come up in your search are spelled very differently. That should be the main take-away for you from the information below.

We would love to convince some of you to study Greek more extensively. If you want to take the next step in really learning Greek grammar, we encourage you to check out all the free videos and student materials at https://bhacademic.bhpublishinggroup.com/beginninggreek/. These materials are keyed to the introductory grammar *Beginning with New Testament Greek: An Introductory Study of the Grammar and Syntax of the New Testament* by Benjamin L. Merkle and Robert L. Plummer (Nashville: B&H Academic, 2020). If you choose to study Greek further on your own or in a small group, we also recommend you check out our "coach in a box" paperback book to accompany your Greek study: *Greek for Life: Strategies for Learning, Retaining and Reviving New Testament Greek* by Benjamin L. Merkle and Robert L. Plummer (Grand Rapids: Baker Academic, 2017).

5.8.1 Greek Nouns

Greek nouns contain much more information than English nouns. How an English *noun* functions in a sentence (for example, as a subject or direct object) is usually communicated by word order. The sentence "The apostle rebuked the demon" means something very different than "The demon rebuked the apostle," even though the same words are used. The word order of the first sentence indicates the *apostle* is the subject of the verb and the *demon* is the *direct object*. Word order is important for communicating the function of words in English.

Imagine that we want to change the English language so that we can put the words in any order. We might say, "Rebuked the demon the apostle." But how would we know which word was the subject and which was the object? We could tweak our language; so we add suffixes (endings) to our English words to let us know what they are doing in a sentence—"SU" for subject, "DO" for direct object, "IO" for indirect object, etc. Thus, we could say and write our new transformed sentence this way: "Rebuked the demonDO the apostleSU." Or, we could say, "The apostleSU the demonDO rebuked." If we all adopted this new system of noun *suffixes*, we could communicate just as clearly, but be liberated from set word order! This is akin to what Greek nouns do. They have a series of *case* endings (suffixes) that inform the hearer or reader how the nouns function in the sentence. A noun listed with all possible case endings for both singular and plural forms is called a "declension" (noun pattern).

The function of Greek nouns depends on the case ending of the noun. For example, the word **φωνή** (voice, sound) communicates that the noun functions as the subject of the sentence whereas **φωνήν** indicates that the noun functions as the direct object. (There are, in fact, many functions of the different cases, but for now, we are going to oversimplify and focus on the main ones.)

It can be helpful to see that English pronouns have distinct forms to communicate different functions in the sentence—similar to Greek nouns with case endings. You would never say, "This is **me** book" (unless you are Scottish, perhaps). The proper way to communicate possession is with the form "my": "This is **my** book."

CASE[7]	FUNCTION	SINGULAR	PLURAL
Nominative	Subject	I	we
Genitive	Possession	my	our
Dative	Indirect object	to me	to us
Accusative	Direct object	me	us

Similar to the distinct spellings of English pronouns, Greek case endings likewise indicate the function of nouns in a sentence (not word order). There are five cases in Greek. (Note that we will only be illustrating four cases here.). The *nominative case* is typically the subject of the verb, answering "who performed the action of the verb?" ("*The Son* of God gave the gift to the man"). The *genitive case* expresses possession or family relationship, which is often indicated by adding "of," answering "whose?" ("The Son *of God* [or *God's* Son] gave the gift to the

[7] S. M. Baugh has a similar chart comparing English pronouns to Greek cases. See *A New Testament Greek Primer*, 3rd ed. (Phillipsburg, NJ: P&R, 2012), 9.

man").[8] The *dative case* often functions as the indirect object of the verb ("The Son of God gave the gift *to the man*").[9] The word "to" or "for" is added to convey this function in English, which answers the question, "to/for whom?" The *accusative case* often functions as the direct object of the verb, answering the question "what?" ("The Son of God gave *the gift* to the man").

CASE	FUNCTION	SINGULAR	PLURAL
Nominative	Subject	φωνή (voice)	φωναί (voices)
Genitive	Possession	φωνῆς (of a voice)	φωνῶν (of voices)
Dative	Indirect Object	φωνῇ (to/for a voice)	φωναῖς (to/for voices)
Accusative	Direct Object	φωνήν (voice)	φωνάς (voices)

5.8.2 Greek Verbs

New Testament Greek has six tenses: present, imperfect, future, aorist, perfect, and pluperfect.[10] The following are examples in the *active voice* and *indicative mood.* Forms of Greek verbs in the indicative mood represent something as certain or asserted ("He went fishing" or "Will he go fishing?"). Statements in the indicative mood do not necessarily indicate an objective fact. By using the indicative mood, the author or speaker is choosing to present his speech as factual, at least for consideration.

TENSE	VERB FORM	TRANSLATION
Present	λύω	"I am loosing" or "I loose"
Imperfect	ἔλυον	"I was loosing"
Future	λύσω	"I will loose"
Aorist	ἔλυσα	"I loosed"
Perfect	λέλυκα	"I have loosed"
Pluperfect	ἐλελύκειν	"I had loosed"

[8] The term in the genitive case will almost always follow the noun that it is modifying (which is often called the head noun). Note too that the genitive has many more functions than indicating possession or relationship (e.g., source, "from").

[9] The dative has many more functions than indicating the indirect object (e.g., instrument, "by/with").

[10] These are sometimes referred to as tense-forms since tense (or "time") is not always conveyed by the form of the verb.

Only in the indicative mood is there any inherent element of time communicated by the verbal form; even then, it is a secondary element of meaning. Beyond the inherent lexical meaning of the verb, the primary element of meaning communicated by both indicative and non-indicative verbal forms is something called verbal aspect.

Verbal Aspect is the subjective perspective or viewpoint from which an author communicates the action of a verb. Although there is an element of time communicated in the indicative mood, in Greek, verbal aspect is the more dominant force of the verb's tense. In English (a time-focused language), the word "tense" is essentially synonymous with time. For that reason, we are tempted to refer to Greek "*tense-forms*" rather than "tenses"—to remind you that time is a secondary element in the indicative verbal forms. In the non-indicative forms, time is completely contextually determined. Yet, conforming to centuries of standard usage, we will usually use the label "tense" by itself.[11] But, please remember that Greek verbs primarily communicate the author's portrayal of an action. Greek is an "aspect prominent" language, unlike English, which is more "time prominent."

Most scholars agree there are three aspects in New Testament Greek.

- **Imperfective Aspect** (present and imperfect tenses): the author depicts the action as ongoing or in process, without attention to the action's beginning or ending. Depending on the context, the action might be depicted as incomplete ("was or is happening"), inceptive ("started to happen"), durative ("continues to happen"), or some other kind of process. One scholar has called the imperfective aspect the "progressive perspective" of the author.[12]
- **Perfective Aspect** (aorist tense): the author depicts the action as complete or as a whole. The beginning and ending of the action (and everything in between) are included in the depiction of the action. The perfective aspect describes a given action simply as occurring or as having occurred without indicating how the action took place ("it happened").

---

[11] In fact, ancient Greek grammarians referred to their tenses as χρόνοι (times).

[12] Robert E. Picirilli, "The Meaning of the Tenses in New Testament Greek: Where Are We?," *Journal of the Evangelical Theological Society* 48 (September 2005): 533–55.

The perfective aspect has been called the "wholistic perspective" of the author. Greek grammarians debate whether the future tense presents action with perfective aspect or is aspectually non-specific. We are inclined to think the future tense should also be understood as conveying perfective aspect.

- **Stative Aspect** (perfect and pluperfect tenses): the author depicts a state of affairs or ongoing relevance resulting from a previous action or state ("it has happened, and it is relevant to the present context"). Depending on the context, there can be more emphasis on the completion of the action or its ongoing relevance. This aspect has also been called the "combinative aspect" because it often combines elements of ongoing (imperfective) relevance with a wholly (perfective) completed past action.

In the indicative mood, tenses include both the time of action *and* the author's perspective on the action (aspect), but the author's perspective (aspect) is primary. In non-indicative mood verbs, however, time drops out with only the aspect remaining. With non-indicative mood verbs, time is communicated by the literary context.

5.8.3 Why Not More Grammar Lessons Like This?

In reading that last section, some of your eyes just glazed over, especially those of you without a strong background in English grammar. Even those who carefully read all the material on verbs, understood it, and are eager to apply it will find themselves inadequately prepared for the complexities of the Greek language.

You must have more in-depth study than can be provided in a quick overview of the Greek grammatical system. A simplistic understanding of Greek grammar equips you to make many interpretive mistakes. For example, let's say after reading the section above, you use an online Bible program to discover that 100 percent of the verbs in the Lord's prayer (Matt 6:9–13) are in the aorist tense. *Amazing*! you think. *Let me apply what I just learned. . . .* Based on what you read above, you conclude that the actions described must have a secondary element of past-time referring, but the aorist verbal forms primarily depict the action "as a whole" (perfective aspect).

Where did you go wrong? Well, first you did not properly note that the forms are non-indicatives. They are in the *imperative mood.*[13] How can an imperative have a past-referring element? Imperatives always refer to the future. (Also, in Greek, an imperative can express a request or command, depending on the context.) Only in the indicative mood does the aorist tense (usually) have a past-time referring element. Secondly, ancient Greek authors overwhelmingly preferred aorist imperative forms in prayers. So, in Matthew 6:9–13, we find the expected stylistic preference, not a decision to highlight one verbal aspect over another.

We want you to learn more Greek grammar, but we don't want you to be mistakenly self-confident before sufficient study. You need to complete both an introductory and intermediate Greek grammar textbook before you are competent to make grammatical observations.

5.9 ADDITIONAL RESOURCES FOR THE GRAMMATICALLY IMPOVERISHED

I (Rob) tell my students that if they are struggling with grammatical terms, I am sympathetic because I grew up in Tennessee, a grammatically impoverished state in America. Thankfully, there are quite a few books available to shore up the weak grammatical knowledge of native English speakers who are studying a foreign language. If this is your struggle, I recommend the following:

- Braun, Frank X. *English Grammar for Language Students: Basic Grammatical Terminology Defined and Alphabetically Arranged*, Reprint: Eugene, OR: Wipf & Stock, 2013. If you want simple definitions (and illustrations) of grammatical terms such as *interjection*, *mood*, *personal pronoun*, *predicate adjective*, and so on, then this 24-page booklet is just what you are looking for.
- Greenwood, Kyle. *Dictionary of English Grammar for Students of Biblical Languages*. Grand Rapids: Zondervan Academic, 2020. Definitions of grammatical terms are given in English. Examples of grammatical constructions are given in Hebrew and Greek, but the author provides English

[13] One of the petitions in the Lord's prayer is in the subjunctive mood, but as a prohibitory subjunctive, it functions as an imperative.

translations with highlighted English words that make it easy for even basic Hebrew or Greek students to follow along.

5.10 VOCABULARY

βαπτίζω	I baptize, immerse, dip (baptize)
θεραπεύω	I heal (therapeutic)
κράζω	I cry out
ἄγγελος	angel, messenger (angel)
μαθητής	disciple, follower (mathematics)
προφήτης	prophet (prophet)
οὐ, οὐκ, οὐχ	no, not (the three forms have no difference in meaning)

5.11 PRACTICE EXERCISES[14]

A. Writing: Practice handwriting and pronouncing your new Greek vocabulary words. Review your old words too. Write out the Greek alphabet from memory.

βαπτίζω	____________________
θεραπεύω	____________________
κράζω	____________________
ἄγγελος	____________________
μαθητής	____________________
προφήτης	____________________
οὐ, οὐκ, οὐχ	____________________

B. Lexicon (#1): Using https://lexicon.katabiblon.com, do a concordance-type search on the following words. (These are the same words you looked up in BDAG in the practice exercises for the previous chapter.) List verse references for every appearance of these words in the GNT and LXX. Click on the verse references in the far-right column to see what additional

[14] Videos featuring a textbook author working through the practice exercises are found at https://www.wordstudiesforeveryone.com. Before accessing those videos, (1) study the material in this chapter and (2) attempt the activities without referring to the videos.

information appears. Remember, the versification of the LXX can be slightly different from English Bibles in some places.

- ἀσέλγεια
- ἐκπίπτω
- καταργέω
- ποιμήν
- τρέχω

C. **Lexicon (#2)**: Using https://lexicon.katabiblon.com, do a concordance-type search on the following words. (These are the same words you looked up in *NIDNTTE* in the practice exercises for the previous chapter.) List verse references for every appearance of these words in the GNT and LXX. Click on the verse references in the far-right column to see what additional information appears. Remember, the versification of the LXX can be slightly different from English Bibles in some places.

- κλέπτω
- οἶκος
- σοφία

CHAPTER 6

/////////////////

BIBLICAL COMMENTARIES AND ENGLISH BIBLE TRANSLATIONS

We recommend watching the video lecture before reading the chapter. The QR code and link to the video can be found on page x.

6.1 OVERVIEW

In this chapter, we will discuss biblical commentaries and English Bible translations, which can both be helpful tools in doing Greek word studies.

6.2 SIGNIFICANCE

God gives to his people in many ways: generously, kindly, lovingly, mercifully. These words that end in *-ly* are all adverbs—words that further nuance some verbal action. The most common ending for an adverb in English is -ly. The most common ending for an adverb in Greek is -ως.

James 1:5 is a well-known text that employs an adverb to further qualify the activity of God's giving:

> But if any of you lacks wisdom, let him ask of God, who gives to all generously (ἁπλῶς) and without reproach, and it will be given to him. (NASB)

Here James describes God as the One "who gives to all generously and without reproach." The Greek word translated "generously" is ἁπλῶς. Though generosity is within the broad semantic range of ἁπλῶς, it more commonly means "unwaveringly" or "without hesitation." In weighing both the linguistic evidence and literary context, most scholarly commentaries on James recognize that "unwaveringly" is a better translation of ἁπλῶς here.[1] Nevertheless, most modern English Bible translations continue to follow the KJV tradition (i.e., "liberally" or "generously"). If we read the verse in context, we see James is contrasting God with the fickle human of verses 6–8. The doubting man is double-minded, unstable, and erratic as a choppy wave in the storm-tossed sea. God, on the other hand, acts with unwavering intent. He does not offer a gift, only to pull it back a moment later. With this in mind, read meditatively through James 1:5–8. Ponder the joy and stability of knowing that we have a God who gives without hesitation, without wavering, without fickleness.[2]

6.3 WHAT IS A COMMENTARY AND WHY USE ONE FOR GREEK WORD STUDIES?

A commentary is an interpretive guidebook written to help modern students of the Scriptures understand and apply the biblical text. Commentaries can be more popular-level or more technical. They can be written from the perspective of a Christian or a skeptic. (Skeptics obviously are not interested in devotional application of the biblical text.) A commentary author's theological commitments and presuppositions can greatly influence their conclusions. Commentaries are usually focused on one particular book or collection of books of the Bible (The Letters of John [1, 2, and 3 John], for example).

We are instructing you on how to complete word studies in this textbook. Why would we discuss or recommend commentaries? Remember that foundational to understanding the specific meaning of a word is literary context. In other words, you need to be able to accurately follow the flow of the biblical author's thought to bring a proper understanding of the literary context into your analysis.

---

[1] Douglas J. Moo writes, "Taken together, then, the evidence suggests that James is not so much highlighting God's generosity in giving as his single, undivided intent to give us those gifts we need to please him" (*The Letter of James*, Pillar New Testament Commentary [Grand Rapids: Eerdmans, 2000], 59).

[2] A portion of this paragraph was adapted from Robert L. Plummer, "James" in *Hebrews–Revelation*, ed. Iain M. Duguid, James M. Hamilton Jr., and Jay Sklar, ESV Expository Commentary, vol. 12 (Wheaton, IL: Crossway, 2018), 229–30.

Some biblical passages are quite straightforward and transparent in meaning. Some are "hard to understand," as Peter notes about some portions of Paul's letters (2 Pet 3:16). If you are studying a particular biblical passage and finding it difficult to discern the author's meaning, wouldn't it be fantastic if a skilled biblical scholar like D. A. Carson or a world-renowned expositor like John Piper joined you for your study and dialogued with you about personal applications or how to teach the text? Of course, that is not going to happen, but through the writings of Carson, Piper, and many others, you have countless trusted mentors. God has gifted people in his church to be teachers of the Word (Eph 4:11–16). How impoverished we are if we do not avail ourselves of the published insights of these gifted teachers!

At the foundational level, if you have not taken a biblical interpretation class or read a book on interpreting the Bible, we recommend you step back and think about your goal when interpreting the Bible. We contend that, in studying any text, you are seeking to understand the inspired biblical author's consciously intended meaning and, at the same time, obediently submitting to implications of that meaning. Of course, God inspired all the biblical authors, so there is also great benefit in tracing the themes that unite the redemptive story of Scripture and find their fulfillment in Christ. For a simple and practical guide to interpreting and applying the Bible, we recommend Robert L. Plummer's *40 Questions About Interpreting the Bible*, 2nd ed. (Grand Rapids: Kregel, 2021).

Once you have an interpretive foundation, where can you find help in understanding particular passages? If you need a bit more help with the meaning, background, literary context, or theological implications of a text, we recommend a traditional NT commentary. You can think of a commentary as a dialogue partner and mentor. New Testament professor Andy Naselli insightfully notes, "Commentaries save us time by providing the historical, linguistic, cultural, canonical, and literary insights that we simply do not have time to mine for ourselves week in and week out. For $35.00 we can benefit from ten years of a scholar's life!"[3] In choosing to employ a commentary, you are recognizing the commentary author's divine gifting to teach, while not thinking the author is infallible. You must be a "Berean Christian" (Acts 17:11), searching the Scriptures to see if what the author has said is indeed the most faithful and convincing

[3] Andy Naselli, "The Best Part about Knowing the Biblical Languages," March 7, 2012, https://andynaselli.com/languages.

interpretation of the biblical text in question. If you are going to be teaching through a particular book of the Bible, it is worth buying four to five of the best commentaries on that book. Which commentaries should you buy? Here is a resource that will help you answer that question:

- https://bestcommentaries.com. This website, developed by John Dyer (ThM, Dallas Theological Seminary), provides the following explanation of its approach:

> Some professors give students their own lists and others recommend the published lists like those created by D. A. Carson, Tremper Longman III, and others. These are all incredibly valuable, but as a web developer, I thought it would be interesting to create an aggregate score of all the ratings in one place.
>
> BestCommentaries.com collects these reviews and ratings along with those of site users with the goal of enabling Bible students at all levels to make good, informed decisions about which commentaries they should purchase. It also provides a constantly updated bibliography of commentaries on each book of the Bible and other subjects. (https://www.bestcommentaries.com/about/)

Depending on how technical the commentary is, it may have extensive discussion of a particular Greek word in which you are interested. Sometimes, however, even detailed commentaries fail to address the questions we have. That is one reason you are studying this book—to be able to go out in the linguistic fields and gather grain for yourself. At the same time, we don't want to be arrogant and neglect the insights of others. If you have access to good commentaries in your study of the Bible, it will benefit you greatly.

There are two relatively new commentary series that go phrase by phrase through the text of the Greek New Testament and thus likely have comments on the meaning of unusual or debated Greek words. They are:

- Exegetical Guide to the Greek New Testament series (B&H Academic)
- Handbook on the Greek Text series (Baylor University Press)

Currently, both series include a good number of published volumes and are headed toward canonical fullness. These volumes have much discussion of Greek grammar that you will not be able to follow, but they are arranged in a verse-by-verse fashion, so it would be easy to skim a section you are studying and find any detailed discussion on the meaning of a Greek word. You might be surprised at how much you can understand. If you are bothered by how many technical Greek grammatical terms you are encountering and want a pocket dictionary for all those terms, then we recommend:

- DeMoss, Matthew S. *Pocket Dictionary for the Study of New Testament Greek*. Downers Grove: InterVarsity, 2001.

6.4 UNDERSTANDING ENGLISH BIBLE TRANSLATIONS

English Bibles can also be helpful for word studies. As we noted in the previous chapter when we investigated the Greek word κραιπάλη, placing differing English translations' renderings of the same Greek word side-by-side can be instructive. It is true that you can now use the best Greek lexicon (BDAG) and best Greek theological lexicon set (*NIDNTTE*), but even the best word study tools are sometimes incomplete or in error. Committees of biblical scholars stand behind most modern English Bible translations. We don't want to neglect their testimony to the meanings of the Greek words we are studying.

Most people reading this book probably do not have a deep understanding of the history or philosophy of English Bible translations. We think it will be beneficial to orient you to these matters. The material below is derived from chapter 7 ("Which Is the Best English Bible Translation?") of *40 Questions about Interpreting the Bible*, a book written by one of the co-authors of your textbook and edited by the other co-author.

6.4.1 The Original Languages of the Bible

The Bible was originally written in three different languages over a period of nearly fifteen hundred years (roughly 1400 BC–AD 90). The OT was written in Hebrew, with a few Aramaic portions. The NT was written in Greek. While sections of the OT had been translated into a few other languages (mainly Greek), as soon as the Christian gospel began to permeate other cultures, the entire Bible was quickly translated into many other languages—Syriac, Coptic, Ethiopic, Latin, and so on.

6.4.2 History of the English Language

Any living language is constantly changing. "Modern English" (as classified by linguists) is a relatively recent phenomenon—just a few hundred years old. The "grandfather language" of English is Old English, the Anglo-Saxon dialect that conquering Germanic tribes brought with them to England in the fifth century AD (The word "English" is derived from "Angles," the name of one of these conquering tribes.) Later, when William the Conqueror defeated the Germanic tribes at the Battle of Hastings (1066), he and his Norman conquerors brought with them a French influence. Allegorically, we might say that the English language's Anglo-Saxon grandfather married a French lady. The "intermarried" Germanic-French language that evolved from the eleventh to the fifteenth centuries is known as "Middle English" (Modern English's metaphorical "father"). Latin, the language of the church for centuries, also had some influence on the development of the English language.

6.4.3 History of the English Bible

While Latin was the official language of the church, a few portions of the Bible were translated into Old English (Anglo-Saxon) from the seventh to the eleventh centuries. In 1382 the famous reforming church leader John Wycliffe (1330–1384) translated the entire Bible into the English of his day (Middle English). The translation was based on the Latin Vulgate and was copied by hand, as the printing press had not yet been introduced to Europe.[4] Followers of Wycliffe continued to call for reform of the church and monarchy based on the biblical truth they were reading. Very quickly, church officials and the king judged the availability of the Bible in English as a threat to the status quo. In 1414, reading the Bible in English became a capital offense (that is, punishable by death). In 1428, Wycliffe's body was exhumed and symbolically burned at the stake.[5]

In 1526, William Tyndale (1494–1536) published the first *printed* (with a printing press) English NT, translated from the Greek original. Tyndale printed these

---

[4] Europeans began using the printing press in 1454. The Chinese, however, were using printing presses long before Europeans.

[5] Definitely the preferred way to be burned at the stake, as a friend once noted.

New Testaments in continental Europe and smuggled them into England. The first complete printed English Bible appeared in 1535. It was called the "Coverdale Bible" because it was published under the leadership of Miles Coverdale, Tyndale's assistant. Tyndale was captured by followers of King Henry VIII, and in 1536, he was strangled and burned at the stake. As he was dying, Tyndale reportedly prayed, "Lord, open the eyes of the King of England." Only one year later, Tyndale's request was granted as the king officially licensed the distribution of an English translation of the Bible. During the next hundred years, many English Bible translations were produced—most of them heavily dependent on Tyndale's seminal work.

EARLY ENGLISH BIBLE TRANSLATIONS

DATE	WORK	DESCRIPTION
1382	Wycliffe Bible	First complete translation (handwritten) of the Bible into English based on the Vulgate.
1526	Tyndale Bible	First printed NT in English based on Greek.
1535	Coverdale Bible	First complete printed English Bible. Relies heavily on Tyndale Bible, German versions, and Vulgate.
1537	Matthew's Bible	Edited by John Rogers. Relies on Tyndale and Coverdale. First licensed English Bible.
1539	The Great Bible	Revised version of Matthew's Bible by Coverdale. Based on Tyndale, Hebrew, and Greek.
1560	Geneva Bible	NT is a revision of Tyndale, and OT is revised based upon the Hebrew. First English Bible with verse divisions. Strongly Calvinistic footnotes.
1568	Bishops Bible	A revision of the Great Bible translated by a committee of Anglican bishops.
1610	Douay-Rheims Bible	Literal rendering of the Vulgate by Roman Catholics.
1611	King James Version	Translated by a committee of scholars.

6.4.4 The Bible in Modern English

During the last one hundred years (and especially the last fifty), many good, reliable, and readable translations have been produced in English. Modern English speakers face a choice unlike any in the history of Bible translation. Rather than ask, "Which translation is best?" it is better to recognize that all translations have strengths and weaknesses. In fact, it is advisable for a Christian to own multiple Bible translations. The only Bible translations we can label as completely bad are those done by sectarian or cultic groups, such as the New World Translation (NWT), the Jehovah's Witnesses translation that attempts to remove scriptural teaching on the deity of Christ.

6.4.5 Approaches to Translation

There are two main approaches to Bible translation, and all translations fall somewhere along the spectrum between these two extremes.[6] On one side is the "functionally equivalent" translation (sometimes called "dynamically equivalent"). This is a translation that seeks to accurately convey the same *meaning* in a new language but is not so concerned about preserving the same number of words or equivalent grammatical constructions. The New Living Translation (NLT) is a good example of a reliable, functionally equivalent translation. On the other end of the spectrum is the "formally-equivalent" translation. This type of translation is very concerned to preserve, as best one can, the number of words and grammatical constructions from the original. Because languages are so different, a formally equivalent translation almost inevitably results in a stilted English style. The New American Standard Bible (NASB) and English Standard Version (ESV) are examples of formally equivalent translations. The New International Version (NIV) and Christian Standard Bible (CSB) fall somewhere in the middle, being more functionally equivalent than the ESV, but more formally equivalent than the NLT. The following chart includes the various translations' approaches.[7]

---

[6] For an excellent treatment of this topic, see Mark L. Strauss, *40 Questions about Bible Translation* (Grand Rapids: Kregel, 2023).

[7] This chart is taken from Clinton Arnold, "It's All Greek to Me: Clearing Up the Confusion about Bible Translations," *Discipleship Journal* 132 (November/December 2002): 35.

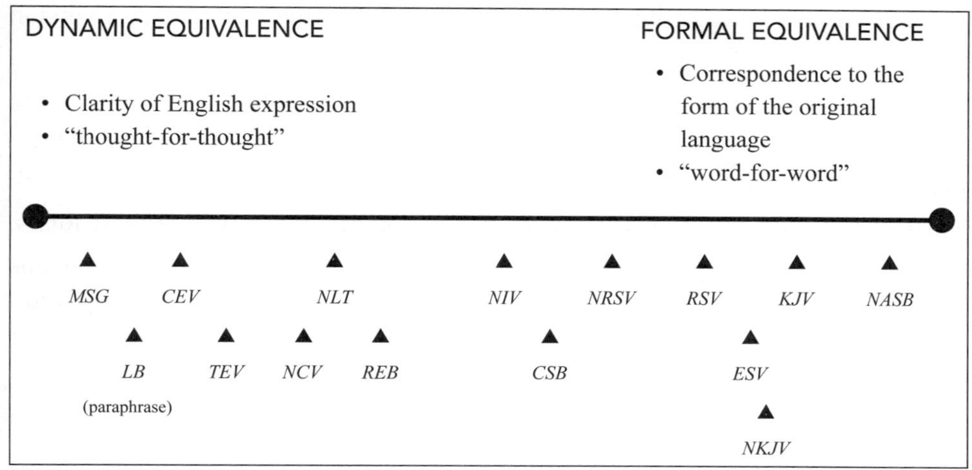

For reading larger portions of Scripture (reading through the Bible in one year, for example), a person might choose a functionally equivalent translation. For careful verse-by-verse study, one might prefer a more formally equivalent translation. In explaining a difficult passage to others in preaching or teaching, it is sometimes helpful to quote other Bible translations which clarify the meaning of the passage. Also, in personal study, reading a passage in multiple translations frequently results in increased comprehension. It is advisable to vary the Bible translation one reads to hear the text afresh. With websites like https://www.biblegateway.com and https://www.biblehub.com, it's effortless to switch between dozens of Bible translations.

6.4.6 Paraphrases

A paraphrase is not really a Bible translation, but an attempt to freely word the meaning of the biblical text. A paraphrase is usually done by one person and allows for more interpretive comments than a functionally equivalent translation. Sometimes a paraphrase seeks to recast the biblical narrative in the setting of a certain sub-culture. *The Word on the Street*, a paraphrase by Rob Lacey, casts the Bible as "urban performance art." Clarence Jordan's famous paraphrase, *The Cotton Patch Version*, sets Jesus's ministry in the Southern United States of the 1950s, replacing Pharisees with white supremacists and Samaritans with African Americans. *The Message*, by Eugene Peterson, seeks to clarify obscure passages and put them in the gritty language of everyday life.

The original Living Bible was a paraphrase of the American Standard Version (a formally equivalent translation completed in 1901) by Kenneth Taylor that he composed for his children during his daily train commute.[8] (The New Living Translation, however, is not a paraphrase but a dynamically equivalent translation.) In contrast to paraphrases, Bible translations are always based on Greek and Hebrew texts and are worked on by large committees of diverse scholars, preventing a narrowness of interpretation and guaranteeing that the work remains a translation rather than veering into an idiosyncratic interpretation or paraphrase.

6.4.7 The King James Version

The best Bible translations are based on the most reliable ancient manuscripts of the Old and New Testaments. The King James Version (KJV) is not highly recommended because it is not based on the best manuscripts and because seventeenth-century English is hard for most modern people to understand. Unfortunately, many hotel Bibles and other give-away Bibles are the KJV translation. While an excellent work for its day, the KJV has been surpassed by many modern translations in both readability and faithfulness to the original manuscripts. Some wrongly and often passionately claim the KJV is a superior translation of the Bible. The historical and linguistic facts do not support this claim.[9] For those who continue to insist on their preference for the KJV, the New King James Version (NKJV) is possibly a better option—being based on the same manuscript tradition of the KJV but updated somewhat in language.

6.4.8 Recent Translation Debates

In recent years, conservative Bible translators have clashed over how to translate generic pronouns and similar constructions. For example, in older English, as well as ancient Greek, the *pronoun* "he" (or αὐτός, in Greek) was frequently used to refer generically to both men and women. Fifty years ago, all English teachers would have said, "If a student wants to speak to me after class, *he* should stay in

---

[8] Paul D. Wegner, *The Journey from Texts to Translations: The Origin and Development of the Bible* (Grand Rapids: Baker, 1999; repr., 2004), 372–73.

[9] See James R. White, *The King James Only Controversy: Can You Trust the Modern Translations?*, rev. ed. (Minneapolis: Bethany, 2009).

the room." Recently, there has been a move in English toward an informal generic "they" or "their" ("If a student wants to speak to me after class, *they* should stay in the room") or the more cumbersome "he or she" ("If a student wants to speak with me after class, *he or she* should stay in the room"). Bible translators debate as to whether translating αὐτός ("he") as "he or she" or ἄνθρωπος ("man") as "person" faithfully conveys the meaning of the original. While the debate can be quite impassioned, the sides are closer than they appear, both acknowledging that much gender-specific language in the Bible was understood by the original recipients as applying to women too. For example, virtually all translators acknowledge that Paul's letters addressed to ἀδελφοί ("brothers") in churches were in reality for all Christians, both men and women. The question remains, however, whether a Bible translation should render the expression ἀδελφοί as "brothers and sisters" or "brothers." Is "brothers and sisters" an interpretation or translation? As one can see, this debate involves the distinction between formally and functionally equivalent translation theory. Scholars favoring the more "gender neutral" translations are usually more inclined toward functionally equivalent translation theory. Those favoring a stricter correspondence of expressions are usually more disposed toward formally equivalent approaches to translation. Conservative Bible-believing scholars, however, are agreed that Greek and Hebrew masculine pronouns for God should be rendered as masculine English pronouns ("he," "his," or "him") because God has revealed himself as Father. For gracious and clear discussions of debated translation issues, see Mark L. Strauss, *40 Questions about Bible Translation* (Grand Rapids: Kregel, 2023) and Dave Brunn, *One Bible, Many Versions: Are All Translations Created Equal?* (Downers Grove: IVP Academic, 2013). As a career Bible translator, Brunn approaches the topic in a winsome and informed way. You can see his overview lecture on Bible translation philosophy at this link:

https://www.youtube.com/watch?v=MxwYK2duyPg

6.5 VOCABULARY

ἀγαπάω	I love
ἀκολουθέω	I follow (acolyte)
γεννάω	I give birth to, bear, beget (genealogy)
καλέω	I call, invite, name (call)
λαλέω	I speak, say (glossolalia)

μαρτυρέω	I testify, bear witness (martyr)
περιπατέω	I walk, live (peripatetic)

6.6 PRACTICE EXERCISES[10]

A. Writing: Practice handwriting and pronouncing your new Greek vocabulary words. Review your old words too. Write out the Greek alphabet from memory.

ἀγαπάω ____________________
ἀκολουθέω ____________________
γεννάω ____________________
καλέω ____________________
λαλέω ____________________
μαρτυρέω ____________________
περιπατέω ____________________

B. Translations: Using https://www.biblehub.com, list the different translations of σπλάγχνα (bowels? inner parts? heart?) in 1 John 3:17. Note that many of the translations are giving a functionally equivalent rendering of the entire phrase κλείσῃ τὰ σπλάγχνα αὐτοῦ ἀπ᾽ αὐτοῦ (lit., *shut his bowels toward him*). This passage is a good reminder that words only convey specific meaning in combination with other words.

C. Commentaries: Choose a book of the NT that you are currently reading, teaching, or planning to read. Go on https://www.bestcommentaries.com and find out the top five recommended commentaries for that book. Do you own any of them? Why not buy one and read it along with your continued study? (Note that when a commentary is labeled "Technical," it will have extensive discussion of Greek grammar.)

---

[10] Videos featuring a textbook author working through the practice exercises are found at https://www.wordstudiesforeveryone.com. Before accessing those videos, you should (1) study the material in this chapter and (2) attempt the activities without reference to the videos.

CHAPTER 7

////////////////////

PRACTICE MAKES PERFECT

We recommend watching the video lecture before reading the chapter. The QR code and link to the video can be found on page x.

7.1 OVERVIEW

In this chapter, we will put together all that you have been learning and give you a simple seven-step method for doing a Greek word study. We will practice this method several times with you.

7.2 SIGNIFICANCE

The prologue of 1 John has many perfect tense verbs. Nevertheless, in the midst of these perfect tenses, we find two aorist verbs—and both appear with less common vocabulary words.

> That which was from the beginning, that which we have heard, that which we have seen with our eyes, that which we **did behold** (ἐθεασάμεθα, aorist), and our hands **did handle** (ἐψηλάφησαν, aorist), concerning the Word of the Life. . . . (1 John 1:1 YLT)

The verb translated "did behold" often has the sense of seeing something with amazement or surprise. The verb translated "did handle," which only occurs four times in the NT, does not convey the idea of a quick touch, but more of a grasping/handling. (You could look these words up in BDAG yourself and see these nuances!)

By shifting both to rarer, more intensive vocabulary words and to the aorist tense, John cues his readers to hear this recollection as distinct from the broader eyewitness reflections of the prologue. To look upon the incarnate deity with wonder and to touch his physical body in sensory confirmation—is this not an unmistakable allusion to Jesus's resurrection (e.g., Luke 24:37–39)?

7.3 A SEVEN-STEP METHOD FOR GREEK WORD STUDIES

It is now time to put together all you have learned. Based on the teaching in the previous chapters, we suggest the following seven-step method as a template for your Greek word studies:

1. **Consider the Literary Context**. Remember that literary context is most important to discern the specific meaning of a word. You should always keep circling back to the context.
2. **Compare English Bible Translations**. Many times, it is in the comparison of English Bible translations that you might be drawn to do a word study. "Why do English translations differ so much in their wording here?" you may ask. Sounds like a text that is ripe for a word study! Comparing English translations can also be helpful in that you are drawing upon the wisdom of multiple translation committees from their study.
3. **List the Greek Word's Range of Meaning**. Access BDAG and *NIDNTTE* to understand a word's range of meaning. Keep a record of your observations.
4. **Note Interesting Appearances of the Word in the GNT**. A concordance-type search via an online GNT or Bible software program will give you every instance of the word in the GNT. Some of these usages might be interesting because they are in a similar context and seem to convey the same idea. Some of the usages may be in very different contexts. Based on the data from a concordance-type search, you may also question if the lexicon you are using has sufficiently summarized a word's range of meaning.
5. **Note Interesting Appearances of the Word Outside the GNT**. At the very least, you should use a concordance-type search to find every instance of the word in the Septuagint. If you own a Bible software program (such

as Logos) that allows you to search the Greek text of Josephus, Philo, or the Apostolic Fathers, you can do that also.

6. **Consult Commentaries**. If you have access to the EGGNT series, the Baylor Handbook series, or academic commentaries, do any of these have any helpful insights to add about the word in question?
7. **Summarize Your Findings**. In light of your research, consider again the context-specific meaning of the word and summarize your conclusions succinctly.

Let's now practice applying this method to a few different words.

7.4 ἀνομία (1 JOHN 3:4): A GREEK WORD STUDY

"Everyone who commits sin practices lawlessness (ἀνομία); and sin is lawlessness [(ἀνομία]" (1 John 3:4).

1. **Consider the Literary Context**. The immediately preceding context is about Jesus's return. Somehow, John's labeling of sin as "lawlessness" is intended to reveal how bad it is and encourage believers not to engage in it.
2. **Compare English Bible Translations**.

VERSION	TRANSLATION
CSB	lawlessness
ESV	lawlessness
KJV	transgression of the law
NET	lawlessness
NIV	breaks the law/lawlessness
NLT	breaking God's law/contrary to the law of God

3. **List the Greek Word's Range of Meaning**.

Insights from BDAG:

- state or condition of being disposed to what is lawless, *lawlessness* . . . characterizes this aeon as Satan's domain. . . .
- the product of a lawless disposition, *a lawless deed*[1]

[1] BDAG, s.v. ανομία, 85.

Insights from *NIDNTTE*:

> Because the word ἀνομία was not found in an initial search of *NIDNTTE*, we looked in the Greek word index at the end of volume 5. For the word ἀνομία, we were referred to the entry for νόμος. There, in the midst of a several-page entry, we read:
>
> Among derivative and compounds [of ἀνομία] the most common is ἀνομία, "unlawful acts, transgression, evil conduct," which occurs over 220x, esp. in Psalms (80x), Ezekiel (49x), and Isaiah (24x); it renders a large number of Heb. terms. . . . It's cognate adj. ἄνομος (over 100x, incl. 20x in Isaiah and 18x in Ezekiel) also stands for many Heb. terms.[2]

4. **Note Interesting Appearances of the Word in the GNT**. The word ἀνομία occurs 15x in the GNT (Matt 7:23; 13:41; 23:28; 24:12; Rom 4:7; 6:19 [2x]; 2 Cor 6:14; 2 Thess 2:3, 7; Titus 2:14; Heb 1:9; 10:17; 1 John 3:4 [2x]). Some of these verses just seem to convey the idea of wrongdoing, sin, or wickedness, but interestingly, several of them are in end-times contexts.
5. **Note Interesting Appearances of the Word Outside the GNT**. A search on ἀνομία in the LXX turns up 228 occurrences. As noted by *NIDNTTE*, the word is quite frequent in the Psalms, referring to wicked behavior or sin.
6. **Consult Commentaries**. In his commentary *The Epistles of John*, I. Howard Marshall has some interesting reflections on the word ἀνομία:

> It seems most likely that the readers were being tempted to regard sin as a matter of indifference: to fall into sin was not a serious matter. . . . According to the traditional understanding of the passage John is saying that sin is a moral (or, rather, an immoral) action, consisting in the breaking of God's law—and that is why it is so serious.[3]

---

[2] *NIDNTTE* 3:405.

[3] I. Howard Marshall, *The Epistles of John*, New International Commentary on the New Testament (Grand Rapids: Eerdmans, 1978), 176.

> In the LXX ἀνομία translates a number of words for "sin," and the link with the law is weak. A number of passages in Jewish texts regard ἀνομία (Heb. *'āwel*, *'awlāh*) as hostility to God in an eschatological context (T. Dan 5:4–5; T. Naph. 4:1; 1QS 1:23f.; 3:18–21; 4:19f., *et al.*).[4]

Marshall compares 1 John 3:4 with 2 Thess 2: 3, 7 and argues that the term ἀνομία emphasizes the "idea of opposition to God which is inherent in disregarding his law."[5] Thus, to commit sin in this context means "to place oneself on the side of the devil and the antichrist and to stand in opposition to Christ."[6] Marshall continues:

> The advantages of taking the word in this way are that it fits in with John's earlier teaching on the presence of antichrists in the world, and that it associates this section of the letter closely with the immediately preceding section: one cannot hope for the appearing of Christ and at the same time persist in the sin which signifies rebellion against him. Sin is not a matter of isolated peccadillos: it is an expression of siding with God's ultimate enemy—the devil (vv. 8–10).[7]

7. **Summarize Your Findings**. The apostle John asserts that sin is not just a matter for indifference but is, in fact, ἀνομία. Perhaps this points to sin as the actual transgression of God's revealed will (i.e., breaking the law), but the frequency of the term in end-times contexts and Marshall's observations point to ἀνομία having a nuance of end-times rebellion against God. In 1 John 3:4, the apostle John asks (in a slight overstatement, perhaps), "Don't you know that to sin is to shake your fist at God in the pattern of the end-times rebellion of the antichrist?"

---

[4] Marshall, 176n3.
[5] Marshall, 177.
[6] Marshall, 176.
[7] Marshall, 177.

7.5 ὑπόδικος (ROM 3:19): A GREEK WORD STUDY

"Now we know that whatever the law says, it speaks to those who are subject to the law, so that every mouth may be shut and the whole world may become subject to God's judgment [ὑπόδικος]" (Rom 3:19).

1. **Consider the Literary Context**. Paul has just finished a chain of OT quotations proving that all persons, both Jew and Gentile, are guilty and without excuse. That none are righteous, no not one.
2. **Compare English Bible Translations**.

VERSION	TRANSLATION
CSB	subject to God's judgment
ESV	held accountable
KJV	guilty
NET	accountable
NIV	accountable
NLT	guilty

3. **List the Greek Word's Range of Meaning**.

Insights from BDAG:

- **pert. to being liable to judgment/punishment, *answerable, accountable***

Insights from *NIDNTTE*:

> Because the word ὑπόδικος was not found in an initial search of *NIDNTTE*, we looked in the Greek word index at the end of volume 5. For the word ὑπόδικος, we were referred to the entry for δίκη. There, at the very end of a several-page entry, we read: "Paul uses ὑπόδικος, 'liable to be brought to trial,' as he concludes his discussion of universal sin: '. . . so that every mouth may be silenced and the whole world held accountable to God' (Rom 3:19)."[8]

---

[8] *NIDNTTE* 1:747.

Due to the slim information on this word, we also consulted *TDNT*. Christian Mauer, in his *TDNT* article, defines ὑπόδικος as "the state of an accused person who cannot reply at the trial initiated against him because he has exhausted all possibilities of refuting the charge against him and averting the condemnation and its consequences that ineluctably follow."[9]

Should the word be rendered "accountable" or "guilty"? The difference is not insignificant. Is Paul, at this point in his argument, asserting that humans are *answerable* to God, or *condemned* by God?

4. **Note Interesting Appearances of the Word in the GNT**. The word ὑπόδικος only occurs one time in the GNT. We wonder how much extra-biblical study of the word linguists did to define it.
5. **Note Interesting Appearances of the Word Outside the GNT**. A search on ὑπόδικος in the LXX turns up zero occurrences.
6. **Consult Commentaries**. Mark Seifrid's careful discussion of this word in his book, *Christ Our Righteousness*, is worth repeating. He offers four reasons why ὑπόδικος is best rendered as "guilty":[10]
   - The sense of "guilt" or "liability to judgment" is normally attached to this word.[11]
   - The preceding chain-citation obviously has to do not with accountability, but with guilt. Since it is fairly clear that Paul continues the thought of this citation when he speaks of "whatever the law says," it is probable that he speaks here of condemnation, not mere "accountability."
   - Paul has just argued that the Gentiles are fully accountable to God without the law (Rom 2:12–16). It hardly makes sense for him to reverse his position and make the law necessary to this accountability.
   - The word [ὑπόδικος] is coupled with the clause, "that every mouth might be closed," an expression which is regularly used in the Scriptures to describe the silencing of the wicked and guilty (Pss 63:11; 107:42; Job 5:16).

---

[9] *TDNT* 8:558.

[10] Enumerated items quoted directly from Mark A. Seifrid, *Christ Our Righteousness: Paul's Theology of Justification*, ed. D. A. Carson, vol. 9 of New Studies in Biblical Theology (Leicester: Apollos, 2000), 61.

[11] Philo, *Spec.* 2.249; Josephus, *Vita* 74 (as cited in Seifrid, *Christ Our Righteousness*, 61).

7. **Summarize Your Findings**. Paul caps off his list of OT scriptures by summarizing that they leave humanity without excuse and ὑπόδικος before God. All things considered, the idea of "guilty" seems best defended by the linguistic evidence. Asserting that humans are simply answerable or accountable to God at this point in Paul's argument would not fit.

7.6 μακάριος (JAS 1:12): A GREEK WORD STUDY

"Blessed [μακάριος] is the one who endures trials, because when he has stood the test he will receive the crown of life that God has promised to those who love him" (Jas 1:12).

1. **Consider the Literary Context**. If we were to mark out the word μακάριος and ask what fits that slot in the literary context, it would be the idea of being favored or accepted by God.
2. **Compare English Bible Translations**.

VERSION	TRANSLATION
CSB	blessed
ESV	blessed
KJV	blessed
NET	happy
NIV	blessed
NLT	God blesses

In James 1:12, does the word μακάριος convey more the idea of subjective happiness/fulfillment (so, apparently, the NET Bible translation) or the more objective idea of being favored by God?

3. **List the Greek Word's Range of Meaning**.

Insights from BDAG:

1. **pert. to being fortunate or happy because of circumstances,** ***fortunate, happy***.
2. **pert. to being esp. favored,** ***blessed, fortunate, happy, privileged,*** fr. a transcendent perspective, the more usual sense (the general Gr-Rom. perspective: one on whom fortune smiles)

a. of humans *privileged recipient of divine favor*[12]

Insights from *NIDNTTE*:

> In the dictionary entry, Silva presents compelling linguistic evidence that the word μακάριος usually has the sense of "happy" or "fortunate," with an emphasis on the pronouncement of divine perspective on reality in various OT examples ("Happy is the man who . . .").[13]

4. **Note Interesting Appearances of the Word in the GNT**. The word μακάριος occurs 50x in the GNT. The beatitudes (Matt 5:1–11) may be the best-known usage. Does a sense of "happiness" or "blessedness" seem to fit the context here better? A sense of being favored by God does seem a bit more natural to the context.
5. **Note Interesting Appearances of the Word Outside the GNT**. A search on μακάριος in the LXX turns up 73 occurrences.
6. **Consult Commentaries**. In his section on James in the *Expositor's Bible Commentary*, Donald W. Burdick writes,

> The expression "Blessed is the man" reveals the author's familiarity with the language of the OT (cf. Pss 1:1; 32:2; 34:8; 84:12; Prov 8:34; Isa 56:2; Jer 17:7) in the beatitudes (Matt 5:3–11). It is not sufficient to translate the word *makarios* as "happy." Even in secular Greek the word described "the transcendent happiness of a life beyond care, labour and death" (*TDNT* 4:362). In biblical usage it speaks of "the distinctive religious joy" which is one of the benefits of salvation (ibid., p. 367). James uses the term to describe the enviable state of the man who does not give up when confronted with trying circumstances but remains strong in faith and devotion to God."[14]

7. **Summarize Your Findings**. Although the non-biblical and LXX usage of μακάριος seem to favor some sense of subjective happiness or delight,

---

[12] BDAG, s.v. μακάριος, 610–11.

[13] *NIDNTTE* 3:207.

[14] Donald W. Burdick, "James," in the *Expositor's Bible Commentary*, vol. 12, ed. Frank E. Gaebelein (Grand Rapids: Zondervan, 1996), digital Pradis version, comments on James 1:12.

the context of James 1:12 fits better the idea of a pronouncement of divine favor or approval. Perhaps there is a sense of, "Happy is the man" in the sense that we can take joy in our position when we know it is in the path of righteousness which is pleasing to God. God's pronouncement of favor rests on us so we can consider ourselves to be happy indeed. Is this trying to pack too much into the word? If "the least meaning is the best meaning," would it simply be better to retain the idea of divine favor (blessed)? Most English translations end up favoring (pun intended) the translation of "blessed."

GLOSSARY OF TERMS

//////////////////

ablaut: a technical term for vowels that change their length (short → long or long → short)

accent marks: marks added to most NT Greek words to aid in correct pronunciation for non-native speakers. There are three accents: (1) acute: ά; (2) grave: ὰ; and (3) circumflex: ᾶ.

accusative case: the case form of a noun (or other substantive) that often functions as the direct object of the verb, answering the question "what" (ἀγαπῶμεν <u>τοὺς ἀδελφούς</u>, "We love <u>the brothers</u>")

active voice: see *voice*

adverb: a word that modifies a verb (e.g., The tall man *quickly* ate his meal).

aorist tense: the Greek tense-form that communicates the perfective aspect (in which the author depicts the action as complete or as a whole). For indicative aorist verbs, the time of the action is typically in the past.

aspect: see *verbal aspect*

article: a word indicating the specificity of a substantive (i.e., a word or phrase that functions as a noun). The word "the" in English is very similar to the Greek article, ὁ (masc.), ἡ (fem.), and τό (neut.).

autographs: the apostolically penned original manuscripts of the New Testament

breathing mark: A mark placed above the first letter or diphthong of every Greek word that begins with a vowel. With a smooth breathing mark (') there is no change in pronunciation, but with a rough breathing mark ('), an "h" sound is added to the beginning of the word (the latter is also added when a Greek word begins with the consonant rho: ῥήτωρ, "speaker").

case: The function of a noun (or other substantive) which is identified by its ending. There are five cases in Greek: nominative, genitive, dative, accusative, and vocative.

cognate: a word whose origin can be traced back to a related word

dative case: The case form of a noun (or other substantive) that often functions as the indirect object of the verb (δὸς δόξαν τῷ θεῷ, "Give glory to God"). The word "to" or "for" is often added to convey this function in English, which answers the question "to/for whom?"

demonstrative pronouns: Pronouns that can be used alone or as modifiers to "point out" (Latin: *demonstrō*) something. There are two types of demonstrative pronouns: near (οὗτος, αὕτη, τοῦτο; "this" [sg.], "these" [pl.]) and far (ἐκεῖνος, -η, -ο; "that" [sg.], "those" [pl.]).

diaeresis mark: two raised dots above the second of two consecutive vowels indicating they are not a diphthong and should be pronounced separately (Κάϊν = Kah-een)

diphthong: two consecutive vowels pronounced as one sound: αι, αυ, ει, ευ, οι, ου, υι

direct object: a noun (or other substantive) that receives the action of a transitive verb

double consonant: a Greek consonant that requires two letters when transliterated into English: θ (th), ξ (xs), φ (ph), χ (ch), and ψ (ps)

eclectic text: a version of the Greek NT that draws from a variety of manuscripts

etymological fallacy: a linguistic (exegetical) fallacy that supposes that knowing the etymology (historical origins) of a word gives us deeper insights into its meaning

etymology: the historical origin of a word

extant: an adjective often used to describe something that is still existing (and not lost to history)

genitive case: The case form of a noun (or other substantive) that often expresses possession or family relationship indicated by adding "of," answering "whose?" (εἰσῆλθεν τὸν ναὸν <u>τοῦ κυρίου</u>, "He entered the temple <u>of the Lord</u>").

gloss: a brief English equivalent of a term from another language

head noun: the noun (or pronoun) that begins or governs a syntactical relationship with another noun—often a noun to which a genitive noun is appended

ideographs: tiny pictures that convey meaning as found in some languages such as Chinese

idiolect: an individual author's personal stylistic patterns

illegitimate totality transfer: a linguistic (exegetical) fallacy of importing a word's entire range of meaning into a specific usage of the term

imperative mood: verbal mood communicating a request or command (e.g., "Go fishing!" "Please, go fishing.").

imperfect tense: The Greek tense-form that communicates the imperfective aspect (where the author depicts the action as ongoing or in process, without attention to the action's beginning or ending). In it, the time of the action is typically in the past.

indicative mood: mood of the verb that represents something as certain or asserted (e.g., "He went fishing." or "Will he go fishing?")

iota subscript: the letter iota (ι) written underneath a (long) vowel: καρδίᾳ, ἀγάπῃ, λόγῳ

lemma: a base (lexical) form of a word that represents all possible forms of a word

lexicon: another word for a dictionary

lexical form: the dictionary (lexicon) form of a word which is the nominative singular for nouns and first-person singular for verbs

majuscule script: the all-capital script found in the earliest extant NT manuscripts that lacks spacing between words and has only rare, erratic punctuation

miniscule script: the lower-case script found in later New Testament manuscripts that includes spaces between words and more regular punctuation

mood: Indicates an author's understanding of the verbal action's relation to reality, i.e., whether the author views the event as factual, possible, desired, commanded, or contingent. The four moods in Greek are indicative, subjunctive, optative, and imperative.

nominative case: the case form of a noun (or other substantive) that often functions as the subject of the verb, answering "Who?" (<u>ὁ θεὸς</u> ἠγάπησεν ἡμᾶς, "<u>God</u> loved us")

noun: a word that refers to a person, place, thing, or idea

perfect tense: The Greek tense-form that usually conveys, in the indicative mood, an action completed in the past that has continuing results. The action itself is no longer being performed, but the consequences of that action still exist in the present (in relation to the time of the author).

pluperfect tense: The Greek tense-form that primarily describes, in the indicative mood, a past state brought about by an action even further in the past. This tense is uncommon, occurring only eighty-six times in the NT.

prefix: a morpheme (sound unit conveying meaning) that is added to the front of the stem

preposition: a word used with a noun or pronoun to clarify that noun's or pronoun's relationship to another word or other words in a sentence

prepositional prefix: a preposition that is attached to the beginning of a verb, forming a compound verb (e.g., ἐκ + βάλλω = <u>ἐκ</u>βάλλω)

pronoun: a word that takes the place of a noun or other substantive, which is called an antecedent

proper noun: a noun that identifies a person, place, or thing and is capitalized in Greek

reverse etymological fallacy: a linguistic (exegetical) fallacy where related or derivative modern words are allowed to shape one's understanding of an earlier word

semantic range: the designated range of meaning of a word

Septuagint: the Greek translation of the OT (from Hebrew and Aramaic)

suffix: a morpheme (sound unit conveying meaning) that is added at the end of a word

tense: A grammatical category usually related to the time an action occurs. In Greek, the tense (or *tense-form*) relates to time only in the indicative mood. New Testament Greek has six main tenses: present, future, imperfect, aorist, perfect, and pluperfect.

tense-form: The present, imperfect, future, aorist, perfect, and pluperfect forms for a Greek verb. These communicate primarily aspect and secondarily time (only in the indicative mood). This book uses the terms "tense" and "tense-form" interchangeably. The term "tense-form" is sometimes preferred as a reminder that, in Greek, time is not the primary element of indicative verbs. Outside the indicative mood, Greek tenses have no inherent time.

text criticism: the study of differing ancient manuscripts with the goal of determining the original wording from which they were derived

transliteration: the writing of one language phonetically (that is, writing out the sounds) with another language's letters or characters

verb: a word that conveys an action or state

verbal aspect: The subjective perspective or viewpoint from which an author communicates the action of a verb. In Greek, the three main aspects are perfective (a wholistic depiction of the action), imperfective (a progressive presentation of the action), or stative (presenting an abiding state that has resulted from a prior action).

BIBLIOGRAPHY

Burer, Michael H., and Jeffrey E. Miller. *A New Reader's Lexicon of the Greek New Testament*. Grand Rapids: Kregel Academic, 2008.

Carson, D. A. *Exegetical Fallacies*. 2nd ed. Grand Rapids: Paternoster; Baker Books, 1996.

Cowan, Steven B., and Terry L. Wilder. *In Defense of the Bible: A Comprehensive Apologetic for the Authority of Scripture*. Nashville: B&H Academic, 2013.

Gallagher, Edmon L., and John D. Meade. *The Biblical Canon Lists from Early Christianity: Texts and Analysis*. Oxford: Oxford University Press, 2017.

Hixson, Elijah and Peter J. Gurry, eds. *Myths and Mistakes in New Testament Textual Criticism*. Downers Grove: IVP Academic, 2019.

Holmes, Michael W. *The Apostolic Fathers: Greek Texts and English Translations*. Grand Rapids: Baker Books, 2007.

Jongkind, Dirk. *An Introduction to the Greek New Testament Produced at Tyndale House, Cambridge*. Wheaton, IL: Crossway, 2019.

Köstenberger, Andreas J., Benjamin L. Merkle, and Robert L. Plummer. *Going Deeper with New Testament Greek: An Intermediate Study of the Grammar and Syntax of the New Testament*. Rev. ed. Nashville: B&H Academic, 2020.

Köstenberger, Andreas J., and Richard D. Patterson. *Invitation to Biblical Interpretation: Exploring the Hermeneutical Triad of History, Literature, and Theology*. Invitation to Theological Studies Series. Grand Rapids: Kregel Academic, 2011.

Kraeling, Carl H., and Robert M. Adams, eds., *City Invincible: A Symposium on Urbanization and Cultural Development in the Ancient Near East*. Chicago: University of Chicago Press, 1960.

Lee, John A. L. *Basics of Greek Accents: Eight Lessons with Exercises*. Grand Rapids: Zondervan, 2018.

Louw, Johannes P., and Eugene Albert Nida. *Greek-English Lexicon of the New Testament: Based on Semantic Domains*. New York: United Bible Societies, 1996.

Lust, Johan, Erik Eynikel, and Katrin Hauspie. *A Greek-English Lexicon of the Septuagint: Revised Edition*. Deutsche Bibelgesellschaft: Stuttgart, 2003.

Merkle, Benjamin L. *Exegetical Gems from Biblical Greek: A Refreshing Guide to Grammar and Interpretation*. Grand Rapids: Baker Academic, 2019.

———. *Exegetical Journeys in Biblical Greek: 90 Days of Guided Reading*. Grand Rapids: Baker Academic, 2023.

———, and Robert L. Plummer. *1 John: A New Testament Greek Reader*. Nashville: B&H Academic, 2024.

———. *Beginning with New Testament Greek: An Introductory Study of the Grammar and Syntax of the New Testament*. Nashville: B&H Academic, 2020.

———. *Greek for Life: Strategies for Learning, Retaining and Reviving New Testament Greek*. Grand Rapids: Baker Academic, 2017.

Metzger, Bruce M., United Bible Societies. *A Textual Commentary on the Greek New Testament (Second Edition): A Companion Volume to the United Bible Societies' Greek New Testament*. 4th rev. ed. London: United Bible Societies, 1994.

———, and Bart D. Ehrman. *The Text of the New Testament: Its Transmission, Corruption, and Restoration*. 4th ed. New York: Oxford University Press, 2005.

Osborne, Grant R. *The Hermeneutical Spiral: A Comprehensive Introduction to Biblical Interpretation*. 2nd ed. Downers Grove: IVP Academic, 2006.

Plummer, Robert L. *40 Questions about Interpreting the Bible*. 2nd ed. 40 Questions Series, edited by Benjamin L. Merkle. Grand Rapids: Kregel Academic, 2021.

Quarles, Charles L. and L. Scott Kellem. *40 Questions about the Text and Canon of the New Testament*. 40 Questions Series, edited by Benjamin L. Merkle. Grand Rapids: Kregel Academic, 2023.

Silva, Moisés. *Biblical Words and Their Meaning: An Introduction to Lexical Semantics*. Rev. and exp. ed. Grand Rapids: Zondervan, 1994.

Wachtel, Klaus, and Michael W. Holmes, eds. *The Textual History of the Greek New Testament: Changing Views in Contemporary Research*. Text Critical Studies 8. Atlanta: SBL, 2011.

Wegner, Paul D. *The Journey from Texts to Translations: The Origin and Development of the Bible*. Grand Rapids: Baker Books, 1999.

White, James R. *The King James Only Controversy: Can You Trust Modern Translations?* 2nd ed. Minneapolis: Bethany House, 2009.